D0811683

# MRS BROWNING

Grylls, Rosalie Glynn

# MRS BROWNING
## The Story of Elizabeth Barrett

### ROSALIE MANDER

WEIDENFELD AND NICOLSON
LONDON

PR
4193
679

Copyright © 1980 by Rosalie Mander

First published in Great Britain by
George Weidenfeld and Nicolson Limited
91 Clapham High Street
London SW4

All rights reserved. No part of this publication may
be reproduced, stored in a retrieval system, or
transmitted, in any form or by any means, electronic,
mechanical, photocopying, recording or otherwise,
without the prior permission of the copyright owner.

ISBN 0 297 77802 1

Printed in Great Britain by
Fakenham Press Limited,
Fakenham, Norfolk

But men will call the golden hour of bliss
'About this time,' or 'shortly after this.'

'Biography' – JOHN MASEFIELD

05231

# CONTENTS

# ILLUSTRATIONS

# 1

# Girlhood at Hope End
## 1809–1832

Hope End, the house in sight of the Malvern Hills where Elizabeth was brought up, was in complete contrast to the character of her father who had had it built. Edward Barrett Moulton-Barrett was an austere man with puritanical standards, while Hope End looked like a 'Kubla Khan' pleasure dome. It had minarets in concrete, turrets in cast iron, and a vast glass dome over the central hall where there was an organ, rich furnishings and stained glass in the windows.

Perhaps the fantastic nature of the building satisfied some buried element of poetry in his nature which was to emerge triumphant in his daughter, Elizabeth. They were a family of scribblers, for the mother Mary (born Graham Clarke) encouraged the children to write verses and herself maintained the literary interests cultivated in her by a devoted governess. Some eccentricities of spelling and punctuation from this remained with Elizabeth all her life.

The Barrett fortune came from slave sugar plantations in Jamaica and some of the harsh elements in Edward Moulton-Barrett's character may have derived from the tradition of a ruling class, confident of unquestioning obedience. With this went a sense of duty to church and state and responsibility for subordinates. Although he demanded obedience, reinforced by daily prayers at home and attendance at chapel three times on Sundays, he was not harsh or unsympathetic as a parent. His children welcomed him warmly when he returned from visits to London where he went on business connected with his Jamaican estates. For the boys there would be games of cricket on the lawn and shooting and fishing in the extensive grounds.

In the family were eight sons and three daughters (a fourth had died in infancy) of whom Elizabeth was the eldest and indulged by her father for her exceptional talents. Born in 1806 at Coxhoe Hall, Northumberland, she was brought to Hope End at the age of three. Christened Elizabeth Barrett,* she was called 'Ba' in the family. They all had nicknames, a sign of unexpected frivolity and tenderness in an otherwise austere environment. Aunt Arabella who came to look after the family on her sister's death, was known as 'Bummy'.

Elizabeth may be said to have 'lisped in numbers' indeed, for at the age of five one of her poems was rewarded by Papa with a ten shilling note wrapped in an envelope addressed to 'the Poet Laureat [sic] of Hope End'. At eight she could read Greek and was always writing or reading. At fifteen she had a poem accepted by the *New Monthly Magazine*, and her 'Death of Lord Byron' appeared in the *Globe & Traveller* when she was eighteen. She said of herself later: 'I could make you laugh, although you would not make the public laugh, by the narrative of nascent odes, epics and didactics crying aloud on obsolete Muses from childish lips.'

At the same time she was a tomboy and in tantrums would throw furniture and ornaments about: 'Ba-lamb could become a tiger.' 'Much more wild and much more mad than the others,' she herself wrote later. A visiting aunt was shocked at the fisticuffs she engaged in with the next in the family, Edward, nicknamed 'Bro'. She had resented his

* Her full name therefore was Elizabeth Barrett Moulton-Barrett.

arrival at first but later he was the object of one of her passionate adorations.

Papa brought her the latest journals from London and fully shared her pleasure when any of them contained contributions by her. He paid for a privately printed edition of her epic, *The Battle of Marathon*, written when she was fourteen, and later for her *Essay on Mind*. She was always grateful to him that he allowed her to share a tutor with Bro for Greek and Latin lessons. He also let her have a free run of his library, though he put an embargo on the shelf where stood *Tom Jones* and Gibbon's *Decline and Fall* which he regarded, not unreasonably, as anti-Christian.

In comparison with others of similar social and economic background, the Barrett girls were treated very liberally. That obedience was exacted they took for granted: Papa knew best and his will must be done. It makes a big difference to be sure that the person in charge does know best and this they did not doubt: it was part of what Elizabeth later looked back on as the 'system', the divine right of fathers. But at the time it was enough for her that she felt Papa was on her side in her reading and her studies, even when he was bound to uphold the judgments of Aunt Arabella. When he arranged for Elizabeth to supervise the younger boys in their classics, it provided a welcome escape from practising the piano or sewing the fine seams that she detested.

She loved Hope End where she had a large room to herself, high up, with stained glass in the windows, and she loved the garden where she tended white roses in a special arbour by the south wall. Years later in her *magnum opus*, *Aurora Leigh* she was to recall the scenery with exactitude. As a child she enjoyed riding until an accident with her pony injured her spine and kept her an invalid for several years but when she recovered she could walk perfectly well in the grounds. There were four hundred acres with a farm, run on 'superior principles', and pleasure grounds designed by

J. C. Loudon who was proud of his work there: 'fruit trees and hops have been planted in quincunx [like the five in playing cards] and in natural form like groups of thickets through the park' and up the 'folded hills'. Elizabeth described the landscape:

> Hills, vales, woods, netted in a silver mist,
> Farms, granges, doubled up among the hills...
> And cottage-chimneys smoking from the woods...

A conventional Victorian pastoral conventionally described, but the girl, unknown and without influence, whose work was accepted by learned journals – and very solemnly learned they were – was to grow into an exceptional Victorian woman; a poet regarded as an equal by the leading literary figures of the day and a wife who liberated herself from individualism and from a father's possessive control.

That was some years ahead: here and now in the 1830s she was happy enough, as the diary she began to keep shows. It is less egocentric than most such productions and, though it indulges in the gentle melancholy made fashionable by an earlier generation of Romantic poets, plenty of humour breaks in when she laughs at herself. She started on 4 June 1831:

> To write a diary, I have thought of very often at far & near distances of time: but how could I write a diary without throwing upon paper my thoughts, all my thoughts – the thoughts of my heart as well as of my head? – & then could I bear to look on *them* after they were written? Adam made fig leaves necessary for the mind, as well as for the body. And such *a* mind as I have! – So very exacting & exclusive & eager & headlong – & strong – & so very, very often wrong.

The reference to Adam is a mild forerunner of the indelicacy of which some critics later accused her.

In another analysis of her character she had written in a memoir earlier: 'I have some resolution to bear pain or to do anything that I wish.... I am not cowardly in the least, on the contrary I can sometimes brave the greatest dangers without fear.'

Sharp comments on friends and neighbours are frequent but never on the family, for she loved them all – Papa and the brothers and sisters who respected, if they could not wholly share, her interests. She tolerated Aunt Bummy who was a well-meaning old dear even when she tiresomely insisted on being accompanied to make conventional afternoon calls on neighbours, leaving the correct visiting cards and staying an exact quarter of an hour. Elizabeth sat quietly in the background, joining in only with perfunctory politeness but all the while registering a strong distaste for these exigencies of 'county' life. Years later she was to write about it to Miss Mitford:

Nothing *can* be so bad – nothing.... This is the way Englishmen grow up to top the world in their peculiar line of respectability.... I wish them all a Happy New Year to abuse one another, or visit each of them his nearest neighbour whom he hates, three times a week, because 'the distance is so convenient' and give great dinners to noble rivalship (venison from the Lord Lieutenant against turbot from London) and talk popularity and game laws by turns to the tenantry and bear down tithes to the rector.

She would have echoed Shelley's phrase, 'I am not wretch enough to tolerate an acquaintance', as she echoed much else of Shelley's, but in actual fact she was not without friends in the neighbourhood.

She divided them into friends and acquaintances, and made a distinction that she kept up all her life between those she liked and those she loved.

One neighbour, Sir Uvedale Price, had been a friend of Charles James Fox. Sheridan and Samuel Rogers had stayed with him at Foxley, for he was good company and had made a reputation by the controversial views on landscaping he expressed in his *Essay on the Picturesque*, which ran into many editions. He and Mr Barrett must have been in agreement in adopting Loudon's landscape schemes, for the expression 'farm buildings upon a superior principle' used in the sales notice meant that they were 'custom-built' to fit in with the landscape and did not merely have Gothic knobbles stuck on cow byres in the style of William Kent. It was Loudon's innovation to have farm buildings contribute to the estate's picturesqueness. To Elizabeth, Sir Uvedale was interesting for his *Essay on the Modern Pronunciation of the Greek and Latin Languages* (1827), in which he anticipated much of the fancy pronunciations of the 1920s. It is a measure of his respect for her scholarship that he invited her to read the proofs of this for him.

But the intellectual among local residents who meant most to her was the blind classical scholar, Hugh Boyd. He sounds a dry stick, but at this time satisfied Elizabeth's educational aspirations and provided an emotional outlet, harmless enough, for one always in love with someone or something.

Among other neighbours, pleasant but of no intellectual interest, was a Mrs James Martin from Colwall with whom she kept up a correspondence which provides information about her later life. A companion – though she would not have tolerated the term – of her own age was Eliza Cliffe, who paid frequent visits in order to paint her portrait; 'tho' it is not a *picture of me*,' wrote Elizabeth in her diary, 'does her infinite credit.' On seeing it Mr Cliffe made the customary remark on portraits that there was something wrong about the mouth, adding, with some insight, that there should have been a book held in front of it.

Sometimes she could escape making small talk and listening to it by pleading discomfort in her back and so win time to read and study at home. She was never tired or out of sorts when it was a question of going to visit the Boyds at Ruby Cottage where she could practise Greek and Latin and argue about philosophical theories.

She had to ask permission each time she wanted to go over there. Sometimes she would be driven in 'the wheelbarrow', as they called the pony trap, and sometimes walk across the Wyche, the pass between the Malvern hills, south of the Worcestershire Beacon. She and her sisters would then have to scramble down a steep bank to the Boyds' garden, a proceeding that Mrs Boyd and her daughter, Annie, thought undignified. Elizabeth described one such visit in the diary. Her sister Arabella led the way:

So down the hill, she bounded; & after her, I bounded; & Henrietta, after me. Down the hill – down the perpendicular – steeper & steeper – into the wood – steeper than steeper! I ran because I could not walk, from one tree to another, half laughing & half crying & half scolding Arabel.

The sisters tactfully went off to find a donkey for the return home and Elizabeth spent a happy hour or so; 'talked about Homer and Virgil, ... *et caeteraes*. ... Donkey came – & I was obliged to go.'

Mrs Boyd and Annie thought Elizabeth's behaviour odd, coming from the big house as she did. She was not bad-looking they considered, with her large eyes and dark hair, abundant though carelessly dressed. Being a blue-stocking it was comforting to know that she would be less likely to rival Annie in the chances of securing a husband in the neighbourhood. Elizabeth, on her side, naturally considered Mr Boyd's wife and daughter unworthy of him and her politeness was often sorely tried when she had to endure their coolness towards her. A diary entry gives an instance:

We set off for Malvern at about half past ten: Henrietta & Eliza riding; Bummy & Arabel & I in the wheelbarrow. ... They drove me nearly to the gate [of Ruby Cottage], & then turning back, left me to make my debut. I could scarcely stand *debout*. Annie, espied in the garden, walked away on catching a glimpse of the carriage. I was shewn into the drawing room – 'sola cum sola' – & was, while I was *consternating* myself, desired to go into Mrs. Boyd's bedroom.... In the midst of our talking, into the room came Annie. Cool reception – on *her* part I mean. Very very cool manner! Mrs. Boyd sent her in to Mr. Boyd to apprize him of my arrival; & in a few minutes, he was ready to see me. When I got into the room, I was at ease in one moment, & in a humour to forget all the worrying out of it.

Mr Boyd's sometimes severe criticism of her writing, as well as his strict standards in translating, were undoubtedly good for Elizabeth who was inclined to dash at things – headstrong, as she admitted herself. There were lighter moments when they played a game that consisted of reading out a line of Greek which he would then put into context. He had a prodigious memory and was, indeed, an able scholar if an unimaginative one. Elizabeth was delighted when he paid her the rare compliment of calling her 'Porsonia', after the famous Richard Porson, the eighteenth-century classicist.

A happy home, beautiful country around, platonic friendship with an older man, appreciation of her talents: it seems Elizabeth had everything she could want, but there was a cloud over Hope End, 'no bigger than a man's hand', but gaining upon it. There were rumours that they might have to leave because Papa's business affairs were going badly. Not only had the abolition of slavery meant losses for all Jamaican estate owners but family disagreements over a will made matters much worse for Mr Moulton-Barrett. It was impossible to know exactly what was happening for he confided in none of the family. They would have liked to know more but they accepted that a father had responsibilities with which he did not worry those dependent on him: that was part of the burden the head of a household must bear, and bear alone.

That Elizabeth with her intelligence and independence of mind should have submitted for so long to the doctrine of paternal omnipotence is surprising to a later generation, but it must be remembered that she was very fond of Papa and that she had the innocence often found in intellectuals. The entries in her diary which read so girlishly were written when she was over twenty-four. Much in advance of her time and of contemporary feminine standards in education, she was a late developer in character. At this crucial time for all of them, her first priority was that Papa should not be worried by questions. Whenever he reproved her, she really considered it hurt him more than her, as on one occasion when he sent her out of the room for slovenliness:

June 17th
After dinner, Papa unfortunately walked *after* me out of the room. . . . The consequence of this was a critique on my down-at-heel shoes; & the end of that, was, my being sent out of the drawing room to put on another pair. So while Anne is mending the only pair I have in the world, I am doing my best to write nonsense & catch cold without any.

# 2

# Family Moves
# 1832–1835

As the year 1831 drew to an end the household at Hope End was understandably in a growing state of tension, made worse by the refusal of Mr Barrett to tell them anything of his plans for their future. 'A fat man with rings' had come from London to take measurements but he provided no information, and gossip from the servants' hall even had it that they were going to live on the Jamaican estates. All they knew for certain was that the house had been advertised for sale in the local paper as a house 'Erected in the Eastern Style of Architecture' suitable for 'A Nobleman, or Family of the First Distinction'. Aunt Bummy and the girls escaped upstairs when sightseers posing as prospective buyers tramped over the lawns and peered in at the windows. Elizabeth wrote in her diary for Sunday, 30 October:

> We cannot persuade Bummy to write to Papa to urge his decisions. . . . Poor dear dear Papa! – may God support him & bless him! – I feel as if I loved him more than I ever did before!

To add to Elizabeth's distress was the indecision of the Boyds who did not intend to stay on at Ruby Cottage after the Barretts left. There was some idea that they would try to find somewhere near to them to live, although this cannot have been very serious considering Mr Barrett had never been neighbourly enough to call nor invite them to Hope End; besides, mother and daughter wanted somewhere lively like Bath.

To keep her mind off her troubles, Elizabeth devoted herself to making a full-length translation of Aeschylus' *Prometheus Bound* in a fortnight, for which she was reprimanded by Mr Boyd who insisted that such haste must make for carelessness. Impetuously she then tried to master Hebrew and succeeded, as she wrote later, 'in getting through the Hebrew Bible from Genesis to Malachi, right through, and was never stopped by the Chaldee'. She was a very quick reader with a strong digestion for tough meat. In addition to readable classics she also got through theological treatises and some natural history (*The Function of Digestion considered with reference to Natural Theology* by William Prout). For light relief she tried two Italian novels, Mary Shelley's *The Last Man* and the current bestseller by Bulwer-Lytton.

When Mr Barrett did come down from London, after an absence of six months, there was relief and a glimmer of hope for he was 'apparently well, & in good spirits'.

He talked to us all day, in his animated agreable [sic] manner; & I could almost believe him to be happy.

Only once his eyes wandered to the window. There were those horrible cows of Capt. Johnson's in the park. His countenance changed; & his eyes were turned away.

But they got no further information from him as to their fate. He told them how in London he had attended a service conducted by the eccentric Edward Irving who claimed to be able to raise spirit-voices. Such a commotion was caused by the sound of the 'unknown tongues' in a chapel containing four thousand people (double the number who could be seated) that it was Mr Barrett himself who leapt on to a bench and shouted above the uproar that it was safer to remain than to risk being crushed in an effort to escape. 'Everybody acquits Mr. Irving of being intentionally decep- tive,' said the readily credulous Elizabeth in a letter to Mr Boyd.

Mr Barrett had also seen friends who shared his views on the Reform Bill then before Parliament, for the early 1830s were times of intense political agitation for the abolition of rotten boroughs and a widening of the franchise. Edward Moulton-Barrett was typical of the new progressives, edu- cated and well-off, who were radicals as against Tories but also as against the Whigs of the old aristocracy. Later they were to become Liberals (always divided into left and right, Radical and Whig) and to maintain their philanthropic and enlightened – or suicidal – tendencies a century later when they introduced death duties and heavy taxation.

In 1832 the Barretts were naturally supporters of Lord John Russell leading the campaign for reform, and Elizabeth was no exception, though she admits in her diary to falling asleep when Bro was reading aloud one of Russell's speeches. 'However I slept only over the calculation of populations. I am not of a *calculating* disposition, in any sense of the word.'

Despotism in the home often went with Liberal beliefs in politics for another element in the make-up of the new radicals was the influence of the nonconformist conscience. This led to plain living with high thinking in many a well- to-do household whose wealth had been founded on principles of strict 'self-help'. That Mr Barrett treated his children as adults when he talked to them of politics or religious controversies contrasts with the way in which he kept them strictly under his control with regard to the provision of money or permission to leave the house with- out his consent.

Again unexpected in one so reserved is the demonstrative affection he shows in letters written from London. Hen- rietta is 'My beloved Daddles', and he spends an extravagant 10d on a franking stamp just to let the family know he is well. 'Remember me to all my beloved ones.' And there is raillery in another which ends: 'I hope that you are all good and gentle and require but very little correction but which whenever necessary I hereby empower Seppy & Occyta to inflict with a bunch of nettles.' Again these nicknames – 'Seppy' or 'Setty' for Septimus the seventh son, and 'Occy' or 'Occyta' for the eighth.

Another paradox in Mr Barrett's mixed-up personality is recorded by a family connection, Sophia Tulk (afterwards Cottrell). As a girl she frequently visited Wimpole Street where the Barretts eventually settled and wrote about the family in an unpublished Memoir.

Elizabeth's father was a very pleasant man in society but a perfect martinet in his own home. The younger daughter one day being asked to join friends at a picnic in the country somewhere near London, went with them in full anticipation of a pleasant day, but her father returning home, enquired where [she] was, & on learning where she had gone, he immediately sent post haste to bring her back.

It seems strange that he allowed visitors to the house – sometimes even without 'vetting' them – so long as none of his children went out unbeknown to him.

By the new year, the Boyds could wait no longer for the Barretts and in May made the move to Bathampton. Between them and Elizabeth were the usual protestations of unaltered friendship when neighbours part: correspondence would be regular and so would visits.

April 23rd
Mr. Boyd pressed me earnestly to go to see him for two or three days – 'There is no harm in asking! – Do ask your Papa.' I was obliged to say 'I will think of it': tho' thinking is vain.
Went away in pouring rain. Left.

So the diary finishes. Four months later Hope End was left.

When it had first been realized that the life at Hope End might continue no longer, Elizabeth had forced herself to think through what it meant to her. In her diary entry for 26 August there is, characteristically, a record of reading Shelley's *Revolt of Islam* and a comparison with Spenser, then apprehension of what a letter from Papa might bring before she makes up her mind to 'consider circumstances'.

I may have to leave this place where I have walked & talked & dreamt in much joy; & where I have heard most beloved voices which I can no more hear, & clasped beloved hands which I can no more clasp: where I have smiled with the living & wept above the dead & where I have read immortal books, & written pleasant thoughts, & known at least one very dear friend – I may have to do this; & it will be sorrow to me. – But let me think of it calmly. I can take with me the dear members of my own family, – & my recollections which, in some cases, were all that was left to me here: I can take my books & my studious tastes, & and above all, the knowledge that '*all things*' whether sorrowful or joyous, 'work together for good to those who love God'. And my dear Papa's mind, – (should *he* not be dearest to me?;) will be more tranquil when he is away from a place so productive of anxieties. There is *one* person, whom it will indeed pain me to leave. But he may follow us, – & in the meantime he will write to me & not forget me. Oh I hope not! To whatever place we go, I will seclude myself there, & try to know & like nobody, – but live with my books & writings & dear family.

The packing took days on end for there was a lot of sorting out to do. Some furniture, most of the silver and a quantity of books, including those collected by Elizabeth on the advice of Mr Boyd, had to be sent into store. She kept with her those that had been gifts. The boys helped their father to knock together boxes from wood that had been cut from their own trees before the auction and stayed behind with him to clear up while Bummy with the girls and maids set off in two carriages (the 'wheelbarrow' abandoned) on Thursday, 23 August 1832.

Their destination was Sidmouth, an up-and-coming watering place of the time, chosen for the sea air which would be good for Ba's cough. The stay was intended to last only a few months but came to three years with several changes of rented houses. The delay was due to Mr Barrett's problems in settling his affairs and finding a suitable house for a permanent family home in London.

The years at Sidmouth were a fallow time for Elizabeth in the story of her life and her literary achievement. She may have been exhausted by her ceaseless working and reading at Hope End, what she herself called 'the precocious scribbling' of her teens. But at Sidmouth, if she was spared visiting now Bummy had left the household, her time was taken up by Mr Boyd's exigencies. He and his wife and daughter moved there in December 1832 but having, as it were, dumped him on Elizabeth's doorstep Mrs Boyd and Annie returned to the delights of Bath.

He, on his side, sensitive no doubt to a wavering in Elizabeth's devotion, irritably complained that her letters were too long for anyone to read out to him and when she cut them down complained that they were too short. After he had been left solitary for four months Elizabeth wrote to protest to Mrs Boyd that if Annie were strong enough to attend parties she could – and should – come to visit her father.

In order to help him with his work on the Christian fathers, Elizabeth's reading was largely devoted now to theological treatises in order to verify references for him. When it appeared, entitled *The Fathers not Papists*, it was a diatribe that would have been inflammatory if it had not been too dull to kindle any attention, and its bigotry upset Elizabeth. Her disillusion with him over this and a subsequent sordid quarrel with the printer over his costs further accelerated the loosening of the ties of their friendship.

Also some of her interest and loyalty was diverted to a minister of the Independent Chapel, George Barrett

Hunter, no relation of the Barretts. Evidently a forceful preacher, he was a prickly churchman who left the chapel but never succeeded in gaining any wider reputation or influential position. He was unlucky, not only in his career but in any hopes he may have cherished of a closer relationship with Elizabeth. She wrote of him years later to Miss Mitford that 'in him the power of suffering is not sufficiently balanced by the energy to act – which produced a dependent character very painful to witness the workings of sometimes, in so dear a friend.' By that time a character had come into her life who had plenty of energy to act.

But if inspiration was running low, a record of the early precocity appeared in 1833: *Prometheus Bound and Miscellaneous Poems*, its publication paid for by her father. She wrote to Mrs Martin on 27 May that 'it came into the light recently. I dare say I shall wish it out of the light before I have done with it' – as indeed she did. She confessed that the rendering of 'Prometheus' into English had been a failure: 'The iambics thrown into blank verse, the lyrics into rhymed octosyllabics and the like – and the whole together as cold as the Caucasus.' In a review the *Athenaeum* advised aspiring translators against trying their hand at Aeschylus: 'they may take warning by the author before us'. Nothing else was noticed.

The miscellaneous poems are mainly verses that in the fashion of the time were ballast necessary to the launching of any poetic venture. There was an elegy on Uvedale Price and another 'To a Boy', with occasional pieces such as 'On the Picture Gallery at Penshurst', 'To Victoria on her Marriage', and verses to 'Earth' and to 'Autumn'.

A discerning critic might have found some presage of quality to come in the sea poems. It was natural she should want to write on new scenes but there is more than perfunctory poetizing in her descriptions. She is original in comparing the obliterating waves with the renewing nature of the hilly countryside she had known:

16

Go, travel 'mid the hills! There, tuneful streams
Are touching myriad stops, invisible.

While the water rides on and on relentlessly,

Wind, stream, no longer sound. Thou shalt behold
Only the pathless sky, and houseless sward;

Boweth the bare broad Heaven. – What view you? sea – and sea!
('A Sea-side Meditation')

She also wrote 'A Night-Watch by the Sea' (see Appendix III) in which she is concerned less with the movement and sound of the waves than with the human reactions of those who may be destroyed by them:

The fisher's widow'd spouse, she watcheth in the house
    To weep – no more to harken!
Loving angels seem to say sweet Amens to those who pray,
    In tones the wave is working—

.    .    .    .    .

While the sick man, dreamingly, takes the rushing of the sea
    For eternity beginning!

By the autumn of 1835 the interval at Sidmouth was over. There had been little to show for it; perhaps an improvement in Elizabeth's health due to the sea air, and certain minor emotional involvements in the break-up of her hero-worship of Mr Boyd and the distraction of a *tendresse* for the Independent minister. Otherwise life for her at thirty was stagnant: she was no longer the prodigy, young and, more remarkable, female, though in appearance she was to strike new friends as remarkably girlish. For all her studiousness her eyes were bright and for all her worrying her skin unlined: a certain immaturity kept her youthful.

Mr Barrett moved the family to London: first to a house in Gloucester Place, then to Wimpole Street. Established there he may have hoped to resume some of the duties of public life which he had enjoyed when he lived at Hope End. In the past when he had paid visits to London there had been interesting political and theological discussions with acquaintances but when he came to live there permanently it was different. He went daily to the City but without the background of estates in the West Indies and the English Midlands he was no one. He had to content himself with the care of his family, and over this depleted kingdom he now began to rule as a tyrant. Was it loss of 'position' and perhaps boredom with his present life that so changed the nature of the affectionate and tolerant father of Hope End days?

Under his roof were the three girls, Elizabeth, Henrietta, the frivolous one, and Arabella, more serious, and his sons, George, Henry and Alfred. Of the others, Edward (Bro) had been sent out to Jamaica in 1834, Sam in 1836 and Charles ('Stormie') in 1840. Elizabeth's favourite, Bro, does not appear to have taken up a profession on his return to England in 1835 nor devoted himself to any other activity. He once distinguished himself as a boy with a speech he gave at a political meeting in Ledbury, and 'he still draws occasionally', wrote Elizabeth, but he must have lacked application. He was the one with most sympathy for Elizabeth's work and, as he was not at all shy, he encouraged her to go out to visit the people that he himself enjoyed meeting.

# 3

# Literary Life in London
# 1835–1838

WITHIN a year life in London had burgeoned. Most important was her friendship with John Kenyon which was to lead to momentous consequences. He was a distant relation of the Barretts and, though not acknowledged by Mr Barrett to the extent of an invitation to dinner, no obstacle was put in the way of his visiting Elizabeth. He was a 'middle-man' of letters; universally liked, he brought together prominent figures of the day but was not ambitious for literary fame himself, content to rest on the unobtrusive laurels that his two books of verse earned for him. He had corresponded with Elizabeth and read her work and was now delighted at the prospect of seeing her and introducing her to established writers who would appreciate her talents.

This was to prove more of a problem than Kenyon had expected; she was too shy to accept his first invitation to meet Wordsworth, but consented to go with him to the Zoological Gardens in company with Mary Russell Mitford. The meeting was the start of a warm and lasting friendship between the two women. Miss Mitford of *Our Village* fame was older by nearly twenty years and senior in the position she held in the literary world. On this excursion to the zoo the three of them went in to watch the diorama (an apparatus that in a darkened room showed revolving scenes) where Elizabeth for the first time looked on the church of Santa Croce in Florence which was to become so familiar to her in later years.

The ice having been broken, Mr Kenyon's gentle and tactful approach secured a promise from Elizabeth to come to his house the next evening when Walter Savage Landor and Wordsworth, soon to be Poet Laureate, were to be among the guests. Perhaps extending the invitation to Bro made all the difference.

The evening was a success. Elizabeth was not disappointed in Wordsworth, though Landor was a far better talker. She did not approve of his boisterousness and 'throat peals of laughter' (Dickens's Boythorn in *Bleak House* was an affectionate caricature), but she called to mind that in his hands 'the ashes of antiquity burn again', and tried to be respectful. She herself was outshone by her brother who dared to beard the great man and abuse him for 'ambitious singularity and affectation'. Bro must have had considerable charm to get away with this, for Landor was not a man to trifle with lightly. Elizabeth summed up the evening: 'I never walked in the skies before: and perhaps never shall again, when so many stars are out.'

It is no wonder that Miss Mitford found her 'a delightful young creature: shy and timid and modest'. In their correspondence the younger woman is at first reverential then on an equality and the intimacy that developed survived disagreements. As in her letters to her sisters, Elizabeth could chat about trivialities, in this case about Flush, the little spaniel that Miss Mitford presented for company in the invalid's sickroom. It was Miss Mitford who provided the description of Elizabeth that has served as a portrait ever since:

Of a slight, delicate figure, with a shower of dark curls falling on either side of a most expressive face, tender eyes, richly fringed by dark eyelashes, a smile like a sunbeam and such a look of youthfulness that I had some difficulty persuading a friend . . . that the translatress of *Prometheus*, the authoress of *The Essay on Mind* was old enough to be introduced into company, in technical language, was 'out'.

This image has remained but it is misleading. In contrast to her gentleness there was a strong Bohemian side to Elizabeth. She felt most at home with mavericks, those who were outside conventional circles.

Meeting literary lions was by no means all that London now afforded Elizabeth. Her work was already known to a few discerning critics and Mr Kenyon wanted to further it. The editors who had accepted her contributions as an unknown young woman from Hope End wanted more and they wanted to meet her personally.

The 1830s were the great days of serious periodical journalism developing from the *Tatler* (1709) and the *Spectator* (1711) in which Steele and Addison had made their names more than a century before. Magazines like *Blackwood's Edinburgh Magazine* and the *London Review* aimed at extending the range of the reviews by printing contemporary poetry and some fiction alongside essays. *Blackwood's* is mostly remembered now for its savaging of Keats – but how many of his admirers ever return to *Hyperion*?

These journals were joined by the revived *Spectator* of 1820, intended to be the voice of 'educated radicalism', and the *Athenaeum*, which reached its zenith under the editorship of Charles Wentworth Dilke who set out to abolish 'puffery' and generally to exact high standards from its contributors and its subscribers. Merged with the *Nation* in 1921, it was submerged by the *New Statesman* in 1931. Others followed, but it was the *Athenaeum* to which Elizabeth and other serious writers paid most attention.

Besides these serious periodicals there now also appeared

lighter occasional productions of the *Keepsake* kind, the coffee-table books of their time, edited by literary-minded society ladies for the idle feminine readership of the middle classes. After meeting Elizabeth, Landor suggested to Lady Blessington that she invite something for the *Keepsake* that, typically, she was about to edit. When Miss Mitford, who did not come into the pin-money category but had to write for a living, undertook some of the Finden *Tableaux* series and asked Elizabeth for a contribution, she obliged with 'The Romaunt of Margret'. When it appeared, the *Athenaeum* picked it out as 'one of the most beautiful things from a woman's hand which has appeared for many a day'.

Encouraged by this and on the advice of Mr Kenyon, Elizabeth decided to publish a volume under her own name in 1838. She collected together her occasional pieces and prefaced them with a long dramatic poem which she entitled *The Seraphim*.

The historical setting for this was the time of the Crucifixion but it soon left *terra firma* for mystical, not to say misty, realms – an early manifestation of the side of Elizabeth's nature attracted to the occult and paranormal. It was acclaimed by the short-lived *Sunbeam* as sustaining a more prolonged flight than Tennyson could have contrived: 'its theme wonderful to be spoken of by men – by an Aeschylus and a Shelley: how much more wonderful thus uttered by a woman!'

The shorter poems were also praised, less immoderately and more valuably, by respected critics: one of them the redoubtable John Wilson (Christopher North) of *Blackwood's*. It was not often that he found things beautiful, or wrote, as he did of 'Isobel's Child', that 'it was beyond all dispute the production of a genius'. The story shows Elizabeth's gift of narrative which was to develop later in her *Aurora Leigh*. A child's deathbed was a favourite Victorian theme in novels and in pictures as was the idea going with it that the child was better off in heaven and that it was selfish of parents to grieve. This is expressed here by Isobel, the bereaved mother, to the nurse.

> I changed the cruel prayer I made,
> And bowed my meekened face, and prayed
> That God would do His will! and thus
> He did it, nurse! He parted *us*.
> And His sun shows victorious
> The dead calm face, – and *I* am calm,
> And Heaven is hearkening a new psalm.

In the early forties the volume appeared in the United States and laid the foundations of a reputation which equalled any she enjoyed in England and brought her later friendships. Two years later, in 1842, she heard from James Russell Lowell who sent her a copy of *A Year's Life* and asked her for a contribution to a magazine he was bringing out in Boston with the customary student aspiration of improving the state of culture there. Responding to this appeal she sent him three poems of which 'The Maiden's Death' appeared in his *Pioneer*.

Fashions in fame are impossible to assess: there are imponderables that one generation cannot explain to another. With regard to Elizabeth, it could be said that once she published under her own name she filled a void in the ranks of women writers: Felicia Hemans was dead, Laetitia Landon out of sight in an African colony where she met a mysterious death, and Christina Rossetti, who is more to the modern taste, was yet to come. But Elizabeth's work was admired while it was still published anonymously and this was due to the fact that she met the demand of the time for moral seriousness sugared with sentimentality. As she developed she outgrew this and allowed acerbity to creep in. Despite her withdrawn way of life she knew the world; one might say in her case that the onlooker saw more of the game. Her social comment in 'The Cry of the Children' and 'The Runaway Slave' influenced public opinion more than any politically minded, socially conscious propaganda. In the remarkable verse-novel, *Aurora Leigh*, she offered many surprises as to her insights, psychological and, if you will, sociological.

Elizabeth always found time for letter-writing. Mr Boyd, now living in north London, was still in correspondence with her and although there is no longer hero-worship in her manner towards him, they still discuss literary matters. She thanks him for 'a copy of *The Pathfinder* (what an excellent name for an American Journal!)' which had a notice of Robert Browning's *A Blot in the 'Scutcheon* – 'I do assure you,' she goes on, 'I never saw him in my life – do not know him even by correspondence and yet, whether through fellow-feeling for the Eleusinian Mysteries, or whether through the more generous motive of appreciation of his powers, I am very sensitive [to hostile criticism of him].'

George Hunter also received sympathy for his reverses, although she was beginning to feel that these were largely self-inflicted. She also found time for lesser lights of the literary world, such as the importunate Richard Hengist Horne who wanted her to collaborate with him on a play.

But the enjoyment of meeting interesting people who admired her, and the success of her book were overcast by her worsened state of health. There have been many speculations about what her weakness really was. In *Creative Malady*, Professor Pickering states that in his opinion she 'suffered from a chronic lung affliction which had dormant phases', but these phases were not recognized, or certainly not encouraged, by the doctors who failed to stand up to Mr Barrett's preference for his daughter as a dependent invalid.

She summed up her condition herself: 'Without any mortal disease, or any disease of equivalent seriousness, I am thrown out of life, out of the ordinary sphere of enjoyment and activity, and made a burden to myself and to others.'

A change of air was the great panacea of the time and so

the doctors advised that she should be sent away from London to the seaside. This would entail some member of the family accompanying her (a maid was not enough), and Mr Barrett demurred at the threatened break-up of his household. At last he was persuaded and, at the end of August 1838, Elizabeth sailed from London Docks to Plymouth, *en route* for Torquay, with Henrietta and George and Bro.

# 4

# The Tragedy at Torquay
# 1838–1841

TORQUAY was a name that Elizabeth afterwards obliterated from her memory, for what began as a holiday for the family with their sister's health as a good excuse for escaping London gloom ended in disaster. They stayed first with an aunt, Mrs Jane Hedley, sister to the late Mrs Barrett, and then moved to Beacon Terrace, a row of houses sheltered by a hill behind, and so close to the harbour that Elizabeth wrote 'whenever the steam packet leaves it or enters it, my bed is shaken with the vibrations'.

The visit lasted three years. During that time each member of the family came down for visits, including Mr Barrett himself, who stayed for several weeks. Elizabeth's health had its ups and downs: at one period she went for walks and even out in a boat, and so far 'tolerated an acquaintance' as to receive gifts of flowers and journals from Theodosia Garrow, afterwards married to Thomas Adolphus Trollope and to be among the circle of friends in Florence. Theodosia contributed a poem to a *Book of Beauty* which included lines on Elizabeth that made her laugh:

> Innocent beings like thee fade with a gentle decay.

Mr Hunter who had a parish near may have come over as there is a record of his daughter, Mary, staying.

In February 1839, Elizabeth seemed so much better that there was no need for anyone to be kept longer from the paternal roof in Wimpole Street as Mr Barrett made clear, but she pleaded so hard with him to allow Bro to stay that he gave in, though declaring that it was very wrong of her to exact such a thing.

The rest of the year was less good for her. She was ordered to remain in her room and then became so attached to it that she was reluctant to leave: 'I did most emphatically abominate and nauseate the going downstairs.' The doctor wanted her to put books away and she did cut down her reading but included the recently published *Essays and Fragments* of Shelley's (given by her father), interspersed as ever with light novels in English or in French. She also defied doctor's orders by reading an edition of Plato bound to look like a novel. Against orders too, she wrote several poems, among them, 'L.E.L.'s Last Question', for she was always attracted to other women poets and particularly to one who had met such a mysterious and unhappy fate. With Bro she must have read and discussed books in the happy relaxation of their youthful days. He seems to have been an unsatisfactory dilettante but his sister's description was kinder: 'not distinguished among men, because the heart was too tender for energy'.

There was a blow to all of them when in February 1840 news came that Sam had died in Jamaica but by May Elizabeth was making an effort to recover from it and not add to her father's troubles, for she wrote to Miss Mitford in feeble handwriting that: 'It would have been very melancholy for poor Papa if he had lost two children by one stroke, would it not?'

By July she was definitely stronger and beginning to wish to return to London: perhaps the others were a little bored with the retired life at Torquay. Anyway on Saturday, the eleventh, Bro planned to go on a sailing trip with some friends that, always sociable, he had made. It was on that

morning that brother and sister had one of their rare disagreements, probably no worse than a nursery scrap that
Elizabeth described as 'a pettish word'. There were the three
young men and a boatman in *La Belle Sauvage* setting off
gaily enough, all 'excellent sailors and familiar with the
coast'. On shore a squall was noted getting up in Babba-
combe Bay and when they did not return by evening this
was thought to have delayed them. But nothing was heard
of them next day either.

For Elizabeth and the sisters who were with her the agony
of waiting was like that other tragic watch – kept by Mary
Shelley and Jane Williams on the balcony of Casa Magni –
that Rossetti described:

> When that mist cleared, O Shelley, what dread veil
> Was rent for thee, to whom far-darkling truth
> Reigned sovereign guide through thy brief ageless youth?

Three days later news came that the boat had foundered and
all had drowned.

Mr Barrett came down to arrange the funeral and had the
body buried in Tor Cemetery. In 'A Night-Watch',
Elizabeth had written the lines:

> But the corpse lies deaf and still, with its feet toward the hill,
> And its ear to the sea-murmur.

She never had the poem republished: it had been too
prophetic.

To her grief was added remorse that the parting from her
beloved brother had been cold. She collapsed utterly and
both her health and her reason were saved by the devotion
of her father. He was 'so kind, so tender' and never
reproached her, for she tortured herself by thinking that she
deserved punishment for having kept Bro in Torquay.
Together father and daughter prayed, 'Thy will be done.'
To those who have never suffered the loss of someone as
·lose as were Elizabeth and her brother it may seem that she

over-reacted, but there was the dagger of remorse to turn in the wound. What is remarkable is her return to normal life with normality: her religious belief, reinforced by her father, and her love of poetry kept some flicker of spirit alive until time could do its healing work, covering over but never dispelling the wound.

By the summer of 1841 she wanted to return home, to leave the site of the tragedy and to make it up in some way to her father for his grief, but her health was too poor to allow her to travel. She was prescribed drugs by the doctors and it says much for her constitution, and perhaps, her will power that she never became 'addicted' to them although taking them for the rest of her life. She recommended to Miss Mitford her 'amreeta draught' for insomnia: 'Muriate of morphine is what I take – what I call my elixir and I take it in a combination with aether and something else.'

Because she was prescribed and regularly took certain drugs it does not say that she was an addict. The terms 'addicted' and 'dependent' have become unreasonably emotive to the present generation. If we could avoid the terms and replace them by 'medicine' or 'medicament' we should get nearer to the true facts of what has been called Elizabeth's 'addiction'. It has been best put by Professor Pickering when he calls her 'a well-balanced addict (as I am for one, or hope I am, in relation to tobacco)'. To have a drink on social occasions is not to be an alcoholic nor to smoke the odd cigarette to be hooked on nicotine. Pickering also points out that since the drug scares of the sixties and seventies, when students became notorious for the drug-taking that led to brain damage and death, doctors have often withheld pain-killing drugs from those that needed them out of exaggerated fears of permanent addiction.

At last, in September, Elizabeth was allowed to make the journey home, travelling on a stretcher and in a conveyance that played the part of an ambulance. It was a carriage 'suspended on a thousand springs', her bed being slid in and out of it like the drawer of a table. On this she was carried with a shawl over her head up to the bedrooms in various inns. She wrote to Miss Mitford that she looked forward to the life of a complete recluse – 'with no more partings – nor meetings which are worse'.

From the sea air and the view over the harbour at Torquay Elizabeth returned to Wimpole Street, whose gloominess she had described when she first saw it as 'Newgate's walls turned inside out'.

The doctors and Mr Barrett considered that complete seclusion was essential to her survival and therefore she must stay in one room away from the dangers of exercise or draughts. There is some doubt about this room: certainly it was two (American three) floors up at the back of the house, but it was large, for besides her own bed there was another for Arabel, who slept there, and a sofa as well as several bookcases. It still had evidence of her earlier, more cheerful, occupation such as the blind she had had put up with 'pictures of a castle, two walls and several peasantry'. 'Papa insults me', she had written to Mrs Martin, 'with the analogy of a back window in a confectioner's shop, but is obviously moved when the sunshine lights up the castle notwithstanding.' In the same letter she tells how a copy of Andrea del Sarto's 'Holy Family' was carried upstairs by Stormie and Alfred for her to see before it was hung over the chimney-piece in the drawing room. She took enough interest in the room on this return to it to stand her busts of Chaucer and of Homer on shelves and to hang on the walls engravings of contemporaries: these included Wordsworth, Carlyle, Tennyson, Browning and Harriet Martineau. The last two were unexpected choices; Browning was hardly known but she already admired in him 'the palpable presence of poetic genius everywhere', and Harriet Martineau was there, Elizabeth declared defiantly, 'because she was a woman and admirable', and also near to Elizabeth's heart, with her interest in anything on the paranormal fringe, because she claimed that she had been cured of cancer by mesmerism.

On the question of whether the windows were sealed, as is generally supposed, there is some doubt, for the ivy which Mr Kenyon gave her, so that she might have something to look at that was green and growing, must have been planted outside, as she speaks of her pleasure at hearing the leaves tap against the glass when the wind stirred it; and, to give the doctors their due for commonsense, it was only cold air they feared for her lungs: fresh air was to come in during the warm months. What is known for certain is that Mr Barrett's room adjoined hers and that he came in every evening to kneel at her bedside and pray with her. She welcomed these visits because together they said 'Thy will be done', and because of her enduring gratitude to him that he had not reproached her for responsibility for the death of Bro.

She was in danger of becoming as neurotic as he was in her anxiety to keep the family under one roof. She resented it when her brothers went on holiday, something that Mr Barrett must have approved in the case of the trip to Alexandria made by Stormie and Henry as it was in a ship belonging to his company.

If no one in the family was allowed to go out, so no one from outside was allowed to come in. At least that was the theory and has become the legend since. Nevertheless there are known exceptions and there must have been others. Florence Nightingale, walking round from Harley Street, delivered flowers personally. Elizabeth described her later at the time of the Crimean War as 'a pretty and accomplished woman, even *learned* she is, and acting greatly on this occasion'. Ellen Heaton from Leeds, later to be a patron of Rossetti's and protégée of Ruskin's, forced a way in and upstairs. Herself rising socially from nonconformist to church, she assured Elizabeth that her poems were appreciated equally by both. 'There's glory!' commented Elizabeth.

There was an exception always for Mr Kenyon whose support at this time was invaluable. He acted as watchdog keeping other visitors at bay (Mr Hunter was allowed to call, presumably on compassionate grounds) and evidently she enjoyed his efforts to keep her informed as to what was happening in the world outside. It was due to his influence that she contributed to literary journals and that in 1844 she was persuaded to publish another volume of poems.

# 5

# Publication of *Poems*, 1844

In her seclusion Elizabeth enjoyed closer friendships through correspondence than do most people who go out and about. 'Getting and spending, we lay waste our powers' (but she would not allow Wordsworth, whom she admired and had liked so much, to call). A new correspondent was the painter, Benjamin Robert Haydon, who presented her with his famous portrait of 'Wordsworth on Helvellyn' for her room. She wrote a sonnet on this which ends:

> A noble vision free,
> Our Haydon's hand hath flung out from the mist!
> No portrait this, with Academic air –
> This is the poet and his poetry.

The most unlucky of artists, his work was admired by friends and some critics and he had abounding self-confidence that over-compensated for his failure. His historical paintings were unfashionable, although later in the century they came in again. He entered the competition for the murals in the newly built Houses of Parliament but was not selected. For one so sensitive, not to say touchy and humourless, it was the last straw when he hired a gallery for an exhibition of his work and, at first buoyed up by the sight of the crowds in the street below, was irretrievably cast down when he found they had come to see not his pictures but the circus dwarf, Tom Thumb, on show in the rooms below. In despair he committed suicide. He left his manuscripts to Elizabeth for sorting and possible publication but she declined the work of a literary executor. It was to Haydon's influence that she owed an education in the appreciation of pictures valuable to her later when she lived in Italy and visited the galleries.

The voluminous letters to Miss Mitford provide much information for these years but even for this friend's sake Elizabeth would not admit H. F. Chorley. He wanted to meet the author whose works he was reviewing in the *Athenaeum*, to which he contributed frequently in consolation for having been passed over for the editorship. Nor did she receive Richard Hengist Horne for whom she undertook a modern rendering of two *Canterbury Tales* for his edition of *Poems of Geoffrey Chaucer Modernised* (hers were the only contributions to receive any praise from the critics). She also wrote some of the biographies for his *New Spirit of the Age*, but was not pleased with the one he himself wrote on her. She thought it made too much of her seclusion, 'shut up in one room for six or seven years', and being 'deeply conscious of the loss of external nature's beauty'. He never saw her, for, when at last she reluctantly made an appointment, he did not keep it as he was too busy preparing to go abroad. He decided to give up literature and after staying in Germany for a time emigrated to Australia.

The most important result of her association with Horne was the inspiration she received for 'The Cry of the Children' from the report of the Commission investigating factory conditions, of which he was a member. These verses tell the piteous tale without false sentiment and without the waste of a word: a piece of social comment that has not since been bettered.

"For, all day, the wheels are droning, turning, –
   Their wind comes in our faces, –
Till our hearts turn, – our head, with pulses burning,
   And the walls turn in their places.

    .    .    .    .    .

'O ye wheels', (breaking out in a mad moaning),
   'Stop! be silent for to-day'!"

Never taught to pray the children nonetheless plead:

  'Our Father', looking upward in the chamber,
    We say softly for a charm.
  We know no other words, except 'Our Father'...

She read voraciously as ever; less deeply perhaps, for there is no record of the classics in these years, but more widely. She enjoyed books of travels, Alexander Kinglake's *Eothen* especially, and at last considered herself old enough to try the forbidden French writers, George Sand and Balzac. Nevertheless she did not tell Papa and felt guilty at Balzac's 'stench' but persevered with him all the same. Balzac embodied the Victorian's idea of French immorality. In Augustus Egg's picture trilogy of 'Past and Present' it is symbolically on a heap of Balzac's novels that the little girls have built the house of cards that is collapsing. George Sand she called 'the greatest female genius the world ever saw', which was a bold – and exaggerated – judgment, but Elizabeth always showed generosity in her praise of other women writers. There may also have been an element here of defiance: a refusal to be shocked.

By 1844 she was prepared to put together enough of her poems, published and new, for presentation to the public and, by the good offices of Mr Kenyon, Edward Moxon undertook to publish it, having at first grumbled that poetry did not pay. The book was to come out in two volumes but when the proofs arrived she found that the first was too short and in order not to upset the balance of the second which she wished to end with 'The Dead Pan', she dashed off the ballad of 'Lady Geraldine's Courtship'.

It is a conventional Cinderella-in-reverse story of the love of a page for a woman above him in rank and had the usual (and unlikely) happy ending of a Victorian novel. It is no better and little worse than other contemporary ballads or ballades, better left to the ages where they belong. Two things however are remarkable about the poem: first, the amount of enthusiasm it aroused in the young Pre-Raphaelite circle who were held 'spellbound' by it, and in new readers like Carlyle and Harriet Martineau. The second is the inclusion of the unknown Browning among the poets that Bartram, the page, reads aloud to Geraldine:

Or at times a modern volume, – Wordsworth's solemn-thoughted idyl,
Howitt's ballad-verse, or Tennyson's enchanted reverie, –
Or from Browning some 'Pomegranate', which, if cut deep down the middle,
Shows a heart within blood-tinctured, of a veined humanity!

Howitt, too, it is odd to find among the immortals, but Elizabeth was often more loyal than discriminating.

As her first published *Poems* in 1838 opened with the epic *The Seraphim*, so these two volumes of 1844 opened with *A Drama of Exile*. This is based on the story of the expulsion of Adam and Eve from the garden of Eden and, much as in the way of *The Seraphim*, contrasts Christian forgiveness with the revenge of the pagan world in Greek drama. Eve is utterly contrite and Adam magnanimously forgives her; in Eve's protestations of her love for him there are faint fore-shadowings of lines to come in *Sonnets from the Portuguese*. The choruses are generally considered a failure and the substitution of 'I wail' for the Greek φεῦ is certainly mono-tonous and unmoving, but there are nevertheless some colourful lines in the lyrics devoted to the spirits. For instance in the animal chorus:

... my young tumbling lions rolled together!
My stag, the river at his fetlocks, poised
Then dipped his antlers through the golden weather ...

Some critics took her to task for her rhyming: one
example from 'A Vision of Poets' shows to what they raised
objection:

He brake in with a voice that mourned:
'To their worth, lady! They are scorned
By men they sing for, till inurned.'

She was before her time: the house of assonance has many
mansions.

There may be trite ballads and trivial occasional verses,
but the volumes that contain 'The Cry of the Children' and
'The Runaway Slave at Pilgrim's Point' established
Elizabeth as a considerable poet. The new note of acid in her
verse acts as a preservative, and sentimentality gives place to
tenderness. In 'The Runaway Slave', for instance, she could
underline the irony that slavery should exist in a land
founded by men seeking freedom.

I stand on the mark beside the shore
    Of the first white pilgrim's bended knee,
Where exile turned to ancestor,
    And God was thanked for liberty;
I have run through the night, my skin is as dark,
    I bend my knee down on this mark ...
    I look on the sky and the sea.

From the land of the spirits pale as dew,
    And round me and round me ye go!
O pilgrims, I have gasped and run
All night long from the whips of one
    Who in your names works sin and woe.

The slave's child by a white man has died and she prepares
to drown herself.

In the name of the white child waiting for me
In the death-dark where we may kiss and agree,
White men, I leave you all curse-free
In my broken heart's disdain!

In 1850 on the death of Wordsworth, her name was talked about as his successor for Poet Laureate. Chorley in the *Athenaeum* said that to have a woman would be 'a graceful compliment to the Sovereign herself'.

These volumes show her interest in American literature, reciprocated in the States. She heads one poem, 'A Rhapsody of Life's Progress', with a line from the *Poems of Man* by Cornelius Mathews. For Mathews, much less known than James Russell Lowell, was one with him in recognizing her talent and had reviewed her in *Arcturus, a Journal of Books and Opinions*. In the *Christian Examiner* she was now rather fulsomely praised by being placed 'in the centre of that constellation of our favourites, Keats, Hood, Sterling, Tennyson, Emerson, Lowell ... in bold imagination, beautiful fancy and tender humanity, she surpasses all other living writers'. But there was one American whose review of these 1844 poems was ambivalent: Edgar Allen Poe. Of the choral songs he wrote: 'We have none of us to be told that a medley of metaphysical recitative sung out of tune ... is not exactly the best material for a poem.' On the other hand he called 'The House of Clouds' and 'The Lost Bower' 'superlatively lovely', and concluded she 'had done more in poetry than any other woman, living or dead'. Elizabeth summed up the notice: 'You would have thought it had been written by a friend and foe, each stark mad with love and hate, and writing the alternate paragraphs.'

# 6

# Browning Comes to Call
## 1845

WHEN Mr Kenyon kept Elizabeth in touch with literary matters and told her about the writers he knew personally in whose work she was interested, he particularly talked about Robert Browning. He would dearly have liked them to meet but he knew that even for him it would be no good to suggest it. If Elizabeth would not allow Wordsworth to call, it was unlikely she would receive someone unknown: a young man, a poet certainly but also a man popular in society – far from a recluse like herself. Her reluctance would be reinforced by a vestige of feminine vanity.

Drained of health and, as she saw herself, of looks, she felt by the same token immune from misconception when she wrote as excitedly as a schoolgirl to Mrs Martin that she had received a letter from Browning, 'which threw me into ecstacies: Browning, the author of *Paracelsus* and King of the Mystics'. In this letter of 10 January 1845, he had written to her of her 'great, living poetry' ... 'I love your verses with all my heart. Into me it has gone, and part of me it has become.'

Browning at this time was thirty-three, witty, handsome and considered something of a dandy because of his taste for lemon-coloured gloves (Matthew Arnold had to live down a similar frivolous image from his undergraduate days at Oxford) and for taking three baths a day. Miss Mitford in her unreasonable prejudice even accused him of being a type of Balzac's *femmelette*.

His father was a merchant with interests like Mr Barrett in the West Indies but without a country gentleman's background, for they lived outside London in the then typically middle-class New Cross. Mr Browning could draw quite well, particularly comic caricatures, and was also interested in music and pictures, taking his son to concerts and frequently to the nearby Dulwich Gallery. Parents and sister, Sarianna, were devoted to Robert and saw to it that he never endured the rigours of a public school nor indeed of a profession. His first poem, the epic *Pauline*, was published anonymously in 1833 when he was twenty-one, the same age at which Elizabeth had published her *Essay on Mind*. *Paracelsus* appeared in 1835 and had immediately delighted Elizabeth. It was praised by Forster in the *New Monthly*, where he put the young poet on a par with Shelley and Coleridge and Wordsworth. Such was this *succès d'estime* that in May 1836 Wordsworth at a dinner proposed Browning's health (in these days of his laureateship Wordsworth was not always walking in solitude 'beneath the trees or by the glimmering lake').

Browning then went travelling abroad. From the deck of the steamer he found inspiration for one of his best-known poems which opens:

Nobly, nobly Cape St. Vincent to the north-west died away;
Sunset ran, one glorious blood-red, reeking into Cadiz Bay.

On his return in 1840 he published *Sordello* but its obscurity put him under a cloud, into obscurity himself. There was a well-known squib which declared that only two lines in the poem were comprehensible and both were untrue: 'Who will, may hear Sordello's story told' and 'Who would, has heard Sordello's story told.' Even his champion Elizabeth had to admit that *Sordello* was not successful, covering her disappointment with the ingenious simile that it was 'like a noble picture with its face to the wall just now – or at least in the shadow'.

Following this setback, Browning, always 'baffled to fight better', determined on writing for the theatre, stretching to the limit his friendship with the actor-manager Macready, who found the plays unactable. In what for him were low spirits, Browning went abroad again and visited Italy in the autumn of 1844. Here he wrote 'The Englishman in Italy' and its companion piece, 'The Italian in England'. Also 'Saul', in some sort a reply to Christopher Smart's 'Song to David' which had long haunted him. These were to appear in *Bells and Pomegranates*, parts III and IV of the series which ran into eight parts, appearing from 1841 to 1846.

It was on his return that he saw what Elizabeth had written about him in 'Lady Geraldine's Courtship' and, with an impetuosity that matched her own, wrote off that first letter in January 1845. Correspondence followed thick and fast with such sympathy between them that it was as early as March that he dared to suggest calling upon her. She put him off: 'You are Paracelsus and I am a recluse.'

But his impetuosity, his will power, was much greater than hers. By 20 May, a Tuesday, she had consented to see him, still keeping an escape route open by providing him rather than herself with a possible excuse: 'If you should not be well, *pray do not* come.'

He came; up those stairs into the darkened room where his hostess lay on a sofa with Flush beside her. He came at 3 p.m. and stayed until 4.30 – unconventionally long for a first call. She reported the visit to Miss Mitford with strict injunctions as to secrecy so as not to offend the others she excluded. She liked him very much – 'looking younger than he is – with natural and not ungraceful manners', and

followed it up, no doubt on Miss Mitford's suspected disapproval:

> Yes, I did not suppose Mr. Browning to be younger – and only
> observed that he did not look older, if so old as I expected – which
> comes, as you say, of the slightness of form and figure.

The next day she told Papa:

> It is most extraordinary how the idea of Mr. Browning does
> beset me. I suppose it is not being used to see strangers in some
> degree – but it haunts me: it is a persecution.

It is surely strange that she talked so openly about a young
gentleman visitor to her father. Was no Victorian convention flouted by receiving a man in a bedroom alone, and for
so long? The Victorians are stranger than we know. Once
she asked Papa if he would like to meet Browning when he
called to which he replied, 'I do not want to see your literary
friends.'

So it might have continued with polite afternoon visits
but Browning soon went too far. He knew that he had
found his life's mission: to devote his life to a remarkable
woman. Superior to himself as she was, he felt that he alone
could sustain her. He had thought himself in love before,
sought to mend a scarred, if not broken, heart by travel, but
this was different; it was love indeed. In his next letter there
was 'wild speaking' – evidently a declaration of love. This
she put by, telling him that he was confusing the woman
and the poet. He replied, ashamed of his behaviour and full
of apology. She accepted it, continued the correspondence
and permitted the weekly visits.

Elizabeth and Browning spoke the same language, as the
letters that passed between them show. At once they had an
easy intimacy, expressing themselves on paper as readily as
in speech. Gradually the love-making in the letters
developed in words completely in harmony, even to their
Eleusinian mysteries. He wrote to her:

I ought to wait, say a week at least, having killed all your mules for you, before I shot down your dogs ... But not being a Phoibos Apollon, you are to know further that when I *did* think I might go modestly on ... ὤμοι let me get out of this slough of a simile, never mind with what dislocated ankles.

To this she replied:

Am I reading the Attic contradiction quite the wrong way? And now will you understand that I should be overjoyed to have revelations from that Portfolio ... however incarnated with blots and penscratches ... to be able to ask impudently of them now? Is that plain?

Probably both of them thought it was. The more obscure to everyone else, the better they understood each other.

Browning disliked the deception involved in their relationship. At a party he had to prevaricate when Mrs Jameson said how much she would like to introduce him to Elizabeth. Anna Jameson was to prove a valued friend to both of them; a 'liberated woman', after leaving her husband she earned her own living by writing on art collections in England and in Europe on which she made herself a recognized expert. Elizabeth, with a more feminine deviousness, in her continued letters to Miss Mitford now, ominously, if her correspondent had but known it, omitted all references to Browning. Her literary gossip became flatter and flatter as one taboo subject alone was occupying her thoughts. She could indulge herself better when she wrote to Mrs Martin whom she was in no danger of meeting in London by saying:

A friend of mine – one of the greatest poets in England – brought me primroses and polyanthuses the other day, as they are grown in Surrey.

The effect of Browning's visits was an improvement in Elizabeth's health and spirits, for she began to go downstairs and occasionally for drives in Regent's Park. Once, for

Browning's sake, she committed the crime of picking a flower to send him: '*Transie de peur* I was ... listening to Arabel's declaration that all gathering of flowers in these gardens is highly improper – and I made her finish her discourse, standing between me and the gardeners – to prove that I was the better for it ...,' she wrote. And with that courage she could call upon at need, she ventured into the East End to buy back Flush, stolen by dog-kidnappers. Henry had refused to go as he said the dog was not worth the price demanded.

But by autumn the doctors declared that she ought not to risk another winter in London and suggested she went to Italy. In September she had enquiries made about passages there with the idea that one of her sisters or a brother might accompany her, but when it came to asking permission from Mr Barrett he refused it. He put on paper a qualified consent to her going but not to be accompanied by one of the family. No one must leave his roof.

She was still not prepared to allow Browning to rescue her. The situation all that winter was tense. Her father gave up the evening prayers at her bedside (did he regret that she was less often in bed?) and was darkly angry when he once passed Browning coming in: what was he doing here so much? Another one who was annoyed at an encounter on the doorstep was Hunter who referred to Browning as her 'New Cross knight'. And when the Hedley family came to stay for their daughter's wedding there was an awkward moment. At dinner her aunt said to Papa,

I have not seen Ba all day – and when I went into her room, to my astonishment a gentleman was sitting there.
'Who was *that*?' said Papa's eyes to Arabel.
'Mr Browning called here to-day,' she answered.

Another time they asked after the 'man of the pomegranates', so she must have talked about him. One can only think that Elizabeth's invalidism and perhaps her age – for any years after thirty were too old for a bride – dispelled suspicions that would normally have been aroused. She was thirty-nine.

To her sisters Elizabeth told the truth, that she had consented one day to marry Browning, but to spare them their father's wrath she kept the secret from her brothers. She also told Mr Boyd but no one else, and tried to discourage old friends like Mr Kenyon coming to see her in case she let out her secret.

# 7

# Marriage and Escape
# 1846

SHE survived that year and into the next, 1846, but in September Papa suddenly announced that the house was to be shut for several weeks for cleaning and during this time they were all to go into the country. This would make flight much more difficult, even if she could bring herself to consider it. Robert was indignant and more impatient than ever, for the doctors persisted in declaring that she must go to a warmer climate before another winter set in. If they waited much longer Robert declared brutally 'till next autumn and the next and the next, Providence would end the waiting'.

The crisis brought conflicting sides of Elizabeth's nature into open war. At once self-willed and used to getting her own way, and, as she had put it in her diary as a girl, brave when she had to be, she was at the same time yielding, certainly in small things. She had always obeyed Papa and those put in authority under him, which at Hope End had meant Aunt Bummy. It was something she had always accepted; but now, for the first time in her life, she was questioning the obedience on which the whole ordering of family life had been based, the 'system'. She hated to think of making Papa unhappy for she could never be grateful enough for the indulgence he had shown her, rare in a father, with regard to her studies and her writing, and the pride he had shown in her fame. Above all for his support at the time of Bro's death. But how could he bear now to put her very life at risk? She could not but compare his selfish obstinacy with someone else's devotion and readiness for self-sacrifice. She was torn in two.

To defy Papa and desert his roof was bad enough but to do it by way of getting married was worse, for he had a hostility towards marriage that she tried to excuse as a 'peculiar tendency'. He was to bring Henrietta literally to her knees when she asked permission to marry William Surtees-Cook and he was an officer in the army and a relation, not a penniless poet. But are any attempts at analysis necessary? It could be said that he was essentially still a slave-owner, or that he was soured by the loss of his money and social status, but was it not simply that he was jealous, like many another parent who has cast off a beloved child on his or her marriage?

Her father's opposition was not the only problem Elizabeth had to face. Was it right to let Robert sacrifice himself to her: he, so active, so virile? Had love come too late for the girl who declared she would never marry, for now she had nothing to offer a husband? She ought to renounce him:

> So farewell thou, whom I have known too late
> To let thee come so near.

The poet had said that in verse but the woman was weak, or was she for the first time strong in a new strength brought to her by Robert? One day she would show him the sonnets she had written to him:

> 'Guess now who holds thee?' – 'Death', I said. But, there
> The silver answer rang, ... 'Not Death, but Love.'

47

No, she would never show them to him because for his own sake he must be sent away. He could not be sacrificed to an invalid who perhaps could not be a real wife, and an outcast rejected by her father and ignored by the dear brothers and sisters who would be ordered to have no more to do with her. And could she bear to leave them?

> If I leave all for thee, wilt thou exchange
> And *be* all to me? Shall I never miss
> Home-talk and blessing and the common kiss
> That comes to each in turn ...

At once independent and yielding, there was another element in her make-up – the chief one – impetuosity. Suddenly she told Robert she would abide by *his* decision: he could get the marriage licence. She lent him her ring with Arabel's hair in it as a pattern for the plain gold one. They would be married at St Marylebone Parish Church on Saturday, 12 September. Only her maid, Wilson, was in the secret for she did not want to compromise anyone in the family.

The awful day came. She was so worn out with the emotional conflicts of the last months and immediate doubts as to the rightness of the course she was taking that she feared she would faint before she reached the street. But she got downstairs and arm-in-arm with Wilson managed to reach a chemist where she bought some sal volatile. This calmed her nerves enough to enable her to continue the walk to the cab rank in Marylebone Road. Here mistress and maid together hired a fly to complete the short journey to the church.

It was a brief ceremony with only Wilson and James Silverthorne, a Browning cousin, for witnesses. Husband and wife parted when they left the church, having agreed not to see each other until everything was arranged for the journey abroad in about a week's time.

Elizabeth, already invigorated through the strength of

her husband, and in what must have been a state of repressed euphoria, sent Wilson home and drove on by herself to Mr Boyd's house in Hampstead. It was like old times, but a world away, that she was kept waiting downstairs before he came to her. Now she had momentous news to tell him, or rather to confirm to the only friend in whom she had confided her intention. He made her pour out glasses of his Cyprus wine and drank the health of the new Porsonia in it, aware that for her it was no longer the nectar she had once loved to share.

She was on edge for Arabel and Henrietta to come to take her home but when she declared herself feeling well enough they made a detour to the heath. Arabel, it seems, did look at her sister suspiciously but ever since her girlhood Elizabeth had had her reticences and the sisters respected them. It is a sign of her sudden maturity that she could accept this anti-climax to an event that was the most important of her life and sought no dramatization of it.

# 8

# First Years in Italy
# 1846–1847

How did they manage, these Victorians and the earlier travellers when they crossed the Channel, without modern plumbing, without tranquillizers, and arrived on the other side to continue their journeys by horse-drawn coaches without springs or heating or, in the summer, air-conditioning? And yet they survived, indeed, to tell the tale, for somehow in the miserable inns they stayed at they managed to write long letters home describing scenery and sightseeing. In July 1814 the Shelleys had run away at five o'clock in the morning from London, thence by boat in a storm to Calais, with Mary exhausted by sea-sickness sleeping on Shelley's knee, and at once on to Paris. Later Dante Gabriel Rossetti and Lizzie, by then his wife, made the crossing for their honeymoon, a day after it had seemed that Lizzie would be too ill to get to the church for the wedding ceremony. They stayed in Paris, not the most salubrious of cities till the 'tin' ran out.

So it was on Saturday night, 19 September, that Elizabeth and Robert with Wilson and Flush embarked for France on their way to Italy. The passage was stormy and they arrived at Le Havre exhausted, but after a day's rest there they went on by *diligence* to Rouen, and after a short respite there on to

Paris. This meant two nights running without sleep but Elizabeth survived, as had Mary and as had Lizzie, and no doubt many another delicate woman of the time.

They arrived in Paris in the morning of Monday, 21 September – not a bad scramble across Europe – where, thankfully, they found Anna Jameson who 'danced with joy' at hearing their news and was only too glad to be of service to them. It is no wonder newly married or eloping couples often took another woman with them to cope with the problems of travel and Elizabeth must surely have needed someone else besides Wilson. Mrs Jameson declared herself in her letters to Lady Byron (with whom, of all people, she had a close friendship) horrified at Elizabeth's appearance. Half-dead she looked, and at once 'nervous, frightened, ashamed, agitated, happy, miserable'. But Anna was soon reassured both as to Robert's really incredible devotion, for she had known him brilliant and ebullient in London drawing rooms, and by Elizabeth's unchanging sweetness. Anna Jameson had a niece with her, Gerardine, on whose behalf she was at first apprehensive at this encounter with the Brownings for fear she should be infected with romantic ideas of elopement. But she soon came to see there was no danger, and the party travelled on together happily. To Orléans, to Bourges, where Elizabeth described the cathedral glass with a Ruskinian touch – 'as if all the sunsets of time had stained the wonderful painted windows' – to Lyons, down the Rhône to Avignon and then from Marseilles by French steamer to Genoa. The discomforts were the magical thrill of Italy. They reached Leghorn and from there went by railroad to Pisa where they intended to find apartments.

It was at Orléans that Elizabeth had to endure the worst ordeal, for her first letters from home arrived there. She opened those from Wimpole Street with apprehension. That from Papa was worse that she had expected. She may have hoped he would relent but he cut her off completely, saying he regarded her as dead and wanted to hear of her no more. He never opened the letters she continued to write to him. With despicable meanness he turned all her books out of her room and put them into store, charging the rental to her.

Her brother George was no better; he declared she had 'sacrificed all delicacy and honour' and left her family 'to bear the weight of sorrow and shame'. The other boys supported him, for in addition to Mr Barrett's pathological disapproval of matrimony, the family took the view that Browning was a fortune-hunter. He was known to have no profession, while Elizabeth had a small inherited income of her own.

In a letter to Henrietta she showed a healthy anger at this: 'I wonder they do not say in Wimpole Street that he married me in order to murder me at leisure.' But the conditioning of thirty years was never wholly to be outgrown and in moods of depression she pined for reconciliation with her father and for some show of affection from her brothers.

In Pisa they spent six months entirely on their own, a honeymoon period that would make or break any marriage, but theirs survived, an indication of how perfectly suited to each other they were, considering the artificial conditions under which they had met. Now they had to face real, everyday life, with no other companionship. It was a colder winter than usual; they were cheated at the shops and Wilson was unwilling to bargain in the market. On their financial position, it must be borne in mind that they were not at all well-off and neither of them had been accustomed to 'making do'. Browning had lived a sheltered domestic life with his parents who had an adequate income but Elizabeth had been brought up in what to outsiders seemed opulence. Although Mr Barrett had not encouraged extravagance, his children had never had to take thought for where their clothes or next meal were to come from. For their first years in Italy the Brownings could only depend on a regular

£200–£300 a year – Elizabeth's income from bonds left her by a relation, with varying amounts from a cargo ship, the *David Lyons*, and from such royalties as she earned. Browning's books brought in nothing. Later an annuity and then a large legacy from Mr Kenyon set their financial worries at rest. To a later generation it seems strange that they kept a maid. At £16 per annum Wilson was considered expensive, but presumably she fulfilled something of the function of a nurse; Elizabeth would not have needed elaborate needlework for her clothes nor much time spent dressing her hair. When they were settled they employed a man-servant as well. In the context of the time this may be compared with the circumstances of Leigh Hunt, the most indigent of journalists, who still took a maid when he and his wife and six children, all penniless, went out to join Byron in Venice.

In one aspect of married life, Elizabeth need not have feared her inadequacy, for on 12 March, when she was taken ill, the doctor found he had to deal with a miscarriage. She must have become pregnant in the first month of marriage.

The Brownings had intended settling in Pisa but found living would be less expensive and the climate better in Florence, so in April 1847 they set off to look for suitable apartments there.* After about three months, first in an hotel and then in temporary rooms, they left for an expedition to Vallombrosa in company with an American journalist, George Curtis. He was one of others with whom they were to make friends who were members of the Massachusetts Brook Farm Community, a homespun ecological commune where 'the weeds were scratched out of the ground to the music of Tennyson or Browning'. The visit to stay at the monastery was cut short when the new abbot refused to allow a woman's presence – 'a petticoat stank in his nostrils'.

On their return the Brownings took an apartment in Casa

* For details of the Brownings' movements see p. 143.

Guidi at the corner of the Via Maggio and the Via Mazetta. But while housekeeping was idyllically easy with all meals sent in from a *trattoria*, well-cooked and cheap, the rent was too high and they left it in October. In the spring of the next year the landlord offered them the rooms unfurnished at a lower price and it is therefore from May 1848 that their association with the house becomes memorable. They occupied the *piano nobile*, that is the first (American second) floor, and above them lived a young couple, David and Eliza Ogilvy, with whom they became friends and correspondents. Mrs Ogilvy was a forerunner of other aspiring women writers who sought out Elizabeth. She had had published *A Book of Highland Minstrelsy*, and *Poems* were to appear later.

Browning enjoyed collecting antique furniture, bric-à-brac and pictures that he picked up in local markets, as he described in 'Old Pictures in Florence'. Some visitors considered the rooms looked like an old curiosity shop, but all those admitted remembered happy evenings spent sitting on the balcony, or in colder weather by the fire, skinning roasted chestnuts as they talked over mulled wine drunk from tumblers. Browning described his wife in the well-known lines from 'By the Fire-side':

> Reading by fire-light, that great brow
> And the spirit-small hand propping it....

At Pisa they had wanted to live retired and only saw Mrs Jameson and her niece who were travelling through, but in Florence they did not refuse to make friends with members of the English and American colony. Curtis was privileged to introduce other Americans, among them Hiram Powers, the sculptor who won considerable fame later for his 'Greek Slave' exhibited at the 1851 Exhibition in London. 'So undressed, yet so refined, even so pensive in sugar-white alabaster,' Henry James described it. There was also George Stillman Hillard from Boston who had reviewed

# POEMS.

BY

ELIZABETH BARRETT ~~BARRETT.~~ *Browning*

AUTHOR OF "THE SERAPHIM," ETC.

*new edition*

"De patrie, et de Dieu, des poètes, de l'âme
Qui s'élève en priant."—VICTOR HUGO.

IN TWO VOLUMES.

VOL. I.

LONDON:
EDWARD MOXON, DOVER STREET.
MDCCCXLIV.

The title page of *Poems, 1844.* Elizabeth has crossed out the surname
'Barrett' and substituted 'Browning'.

Portrait of Elizabeth painted in 1851 by Buchanan Read, the American poet and painter. It was he who introduced the Rossetti brothers to the Brownings in London.

This sketch by Thackeray must have been done in Rome in the winter of 1853/4, when Thackeray and his daughters were staying there. Mrs Browning is on the right, and the lady on the left is probably Mrs Butler (Fanny Kemble), whom he is escorting to a ball.

Portrait of Elizabeth by E. F. Bridell, Rome 1858. Elizabeth said of this, 'She draws well and has been very successful with the hair at least . . . She comes here for an hour in the morning to execute me.'

From a photograph of
Elizabeth, taken at Le Havre in
1858. An engraving was made
from this for the fourth edition
of *Aurora Leigh*, 1859.

BELOW LEFT Robert Browning
by D. G. Rossetti, London
1855. On first meeting him in
1851 Rossetti said of
Browning: 'His head is most
stunning and even handsome
in the common sense of the
term.'

BELOW Bust of Penini
Browning by Alexander
Munro, 1858, shown at the
Royal Academy in 1859. 'It is
beautiful and *tale quale*,'
Elizabeth said in a letter to
Mrs Ogilvy.

Elizabeth found this portrait by Field Talfourd (1859) 'too flattering — much idealised in fact — but there must be a good deal of likeness or it would not strike so universally.'

Sophia Eckley commissioned this painting of Elizabeth by Michele
Gordigiani (1859), but the first version did not please the Brownings and
was completely repainted, much to the chagrin of Mrs Eckley. It was
Browning's favourite portrait of his wife.

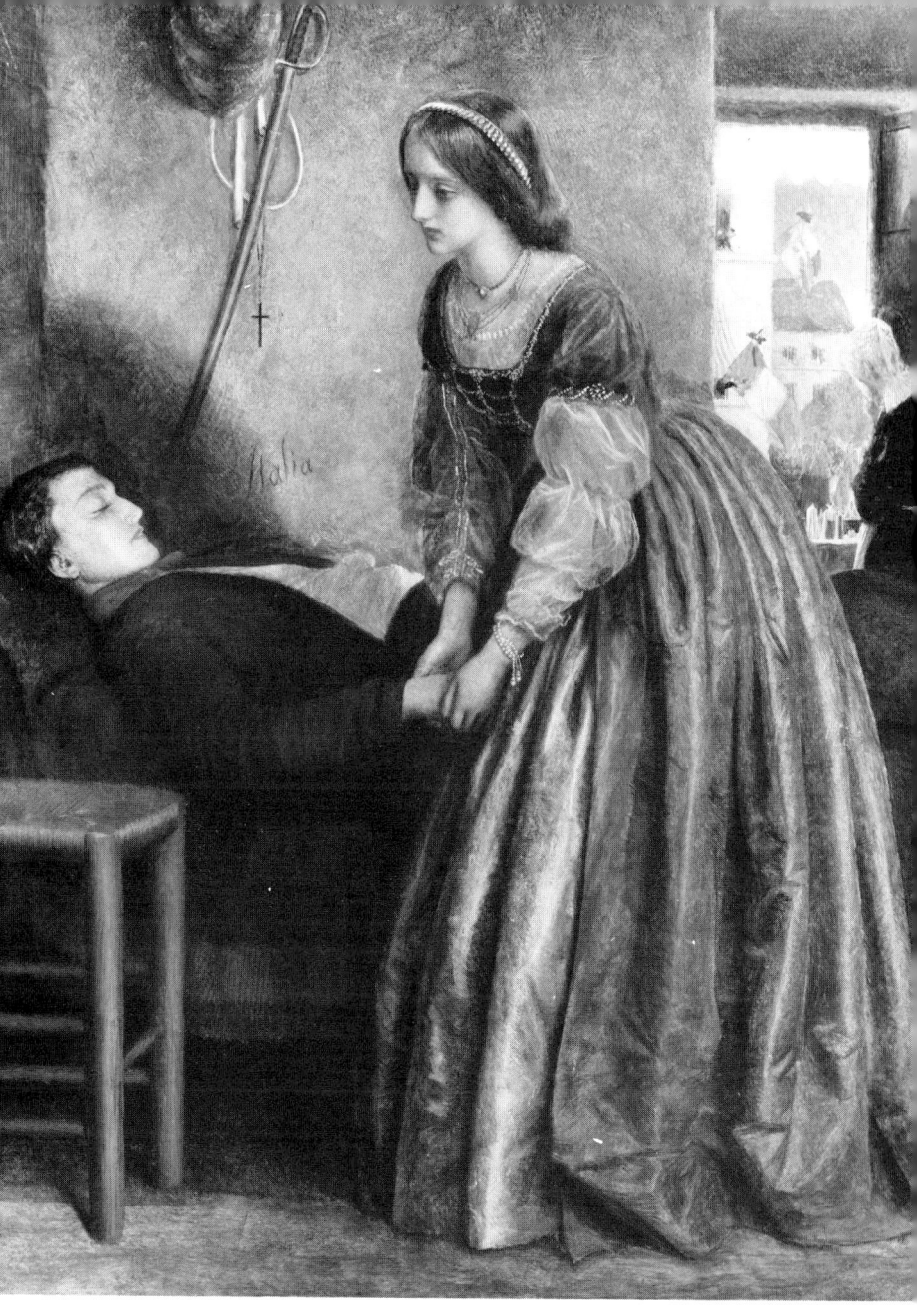

'That was a Piedmontese', by Arthur Hughes, 1860, an illustration to the poem 'A Court Lady' from *Poems before Congress*. The painting, which was commissioned by Ellen Heaton, was adversely criticised by Ruskin who complained that the woman's diamonds did not flash.

TO THE MEMORY OF
**EDWARD MOULTON BARRETT,**
WHO DIED APRIL 17TH 1857, AGED 71.
AND **MARY MOULTON BARRETT**, HIS WIFE,
WHO DIED OCTOBER 1ST 1828, AGED 48.
ALSO **MARY**, DAUGHTER OF THE ABOVE,
WHO DIED MARCH 16TH 1814, AGED 4.

Memorial to Mr Barrett by J. G. Lough in Ledbury Parish Church, Herefordshire.

Elizabeth's poems and was engaged in writing his *Six Months in Italy*. In this he records:

One of my most delightful associations was meeting the Brownings – a happier home and a more perfect union than theirs, it is not easy to imagine – Browning's conversation is like the poetry of Chaucer ... his countenance is full of vigour, freshness and refined power – Mrs. Browning is in many respects the correlative of her husband. As he is full of manly power, so she is the type of the most sensitive and delicate womanhood. Her figure is slight, her countenance expressive of genius and sensibility, shaded by a veil of long brown locks. I have never seen a human frame which seemed so nearly a transparent veil for a celestial and immortal spirit.

One evening the Brownings went out to dinner to meet the Hoppners, an invitation which Elizabeth consented to accept as she was eager to hear their first-hand memories of the Shelleys and Claire Clairmont. They had taken an active, and later a mischievous, part in Byron's adoption of his child by Claire, the unfortunate Allegra. Mrs Hoppner mocked Shelley's vegetarianism and recounted how she had tricked him into eating some roast beef.

Early among the English residents they met were Thomas Adolphus Trollope, elder brother of the novelist, Anthony. He and his wife, Theodosia, were ardent supporters of the Italian revolutionary movement; her articles on it, collected as *Social Aspects of the Italian Revolution* were considered very useful propaganda for the cause. The Trollopes' formidable mother, Frances, lived with them in Villino Trollope. 'She lives in great style here and is very polite to the Americans,' declared Buchanan Read in Florence on his travels. Mrs Trollope was able to rest on very satisfactory financial laurels from the vast output of novels that followed her notoriously cantankerous – and successful – *Life among the Americans* of 1832. She did not spare her own fellow countrymen when they came abroad to save money and to find husbands with glamorous-sounding titles among foreign aristocrats. Society in Italy was not entirely the 'nest of singing birds' that literary and artistic expatriates make it seem. Mrs Trollope's novel, *The Roberts on their Travels*, deals satirically with a family of empty-headed daughters and a social-climbing brother who have to make a moonlight flit when their money runs out, while their quiet travelling companion, who visits the Colosseum daily and reads *Corinne*, happily marries a solid English cousin.

The Brownings were forced out of superficial enjoyments by the tragedy that befell Sophia Tulk now married to a childhood neighbour, Henry Cottrell, who was made a count by the Duke of Lucca to whom he had become chamberlain. Their child of three years old was suddenly taken ill and when she died, it was Robert, full of kindness and energy, who undertook the funeral arrangements for the distraught parents. Elizabeth's verses on 'A Child's Grave at Florence' refer to this:

> And here, among the English tombs,
> In Tuscan ground we lay her,
> While the blue Tuscan sky endomes
> Our English words of prayer.

Sophia must have been sympathetic to Elizabeth for she shared her interest in the occult. Her father had investigated cases of mesmerism and she herself was to attend seances at the Trollopes.

The term 'colony' would be appropriate for the circle of English and American expatriates who were, in fact, the 'wasps' of their time. It is noticeable that such Italians as they knew were married to English or Americans: the Marchesa d'Ossoli, for instance, or the Liberal senator, Professor Pasquale Villari.

G. S. Hillard comments on the English:

The English, indeed, are the true Romans ... they are law-makers, road-makers and bridge-builders, and in their personal habits, the same love of bathing, a taste which has quite died out upon the soil of Rome... they carry England with them wherever they go – even to clothes; his shooting jacket, checked trousers, and brown gaiters proclaim his nationality before he begins to speak; he rarely yields to the seduction of a moustache; he is inflexibly loyal to tea; and will make a hard fight before consenting to dine at an earlier hour than five.

In comparing the Anglo-Saxon Protestants, Hillard goes on:

The most ignorant men I saw on the Continent were Englishmen. No American would be found upon the soil of Europe so profoundly ignorant, though he might have left home with as little knowledge, he would have bolted the contents of half-a-dozen guide-books on the voyage.

On the other side, the English had reservations on American brashness. Elizabeth was gratified to find in Harriet Beecher Stowe 'no rampant Americanisms', and later condescended to declare that Elizabeth Kinney was 'not especially refined for an Ambassador's wife, but natural and apparently warm-hearted'.

As to the natives, Elizabeth writes of their friendliness. Their noisiness was charming in its abandon, so long as it did not keep the visitors awake at night. With typically patronizing English liberalism, she attributes their irresponsibility to lack of political freedom. Soon she was to involve herself enthusiastically in their fight for liberation but first she had to get acclimatized to her new domestic life.

On their honeymoon Anna Jameson had thought them babes in the wood so far as making practical arrangements was concerned but she could now report (again to Lady Byron) that in health and appearance Elizabeth was not '*improved* but *transformed*', and she approved their housekeeping. Wilson settled down after her first shock at the nude statues: 'She thinks she will try again, and the troublesome modesty may subside,' Elizabeth wrote to Henrietta. She could also tell her that she was enjoying health not known since her early girlhood: Flush was no longer required to eat up dinners for her. She went round art galleries, visited churches and took walks along the Arno.

I have seen the Venus. I have seen the divine Raphaels. I have stood by Michael Angelo's tomb in Santa Croce. I have looked at the wonderful Duomo. At Pisa we say 'How beautiful!', here we say nothing: it is enough if we can breathe.

# 9

# Reactions to the Risorgimento
# 1848

THE English attitude to foreign affairs is paradoxical. There are those to whom anything further across the Channel than France is a 'far off country about which we know nothing' and care less, and there are those who adopt a favourite country, become experts on it and even go out and fight in its wars. H. A. L. Fisher wrote of this in his *History of Europe*:

> No other country in Europe so swiftly or lightly conceives a passion for the oppressed in other lands. Pro-Vaudois, Pro-Catalan, Pro-Slav, Pro-Hellenic, Pro-Italian, Pro-Bulgar, Pro-Armenian, Pro-Serb, Pro-Boer, Pro-Belgian. The English idealist, reckoning little of material profit or loss, helps in shaping the policy of his country and can never be wholly neglected.

Liberation has often meant greater tyranny – 'Methinks there will a worse come in his place.' The list of oppressed nationalities can be updated and some of them put into reverse; pro-Boers are now anti-Afrikaners. And Austria after the 1914–18 war lost an empire but found a role in romance. Musicals were composed with Vienna for a setting and the edelweiss became the most *gemütlich* of plants. It is only the Italian natives of the parts of the Tyrol that used to belong to them as Alto Adige who still see Austrians in a different light, the *tedeschi* of the old empire.

There had been uprisings of subject races in Europe ever since the Napoleonic Wars; for, paradoxically, it was his conquests, with their usually liberal constitutions to follow, that roused the spirit of latent nationalism. Poland in 1815 in its revolt against Russia and Prussia produced the first of the patriotic leader-heroes, Kosciusko. Typical of British sympathizers, Thomas Campbell wrote, 'And Freedom shrieked – as Kosciusko fell,' and Shelley took lodgings in Poland Street, London, to show solidarity.

In Hungary also there emerged another hero of the same type, Louis Kossuth, who in the spring of 1848 led the revolt against domination from Vienna.

Best known to English history is the Greek War of Independence because of Byron's romantic contribution to it by dying at Missolonghi in 1824. He and Shelley had both supported the Italian revolt of the 1820s. Now, in 1846, these smouldering fires were bursting into flame again.

A new pope, Pius IX (Pio Nono) was hailed as a liberal successor to the tyrannical Gregory XVI who had ruled the subjects of his Papal States with the guns of the Austrian troops in occupation of most of the north of the country. There was a war on two fronts to be fought, against the foreign Austrians and against an indigenous institution, the Papal States with temporal power. The hopes of Italian rebels and of sympathetic onlookers in 1848 therefore were focused on Pio Nono for reforms in Rome and on Louis Napoleon, president of the French Republic and later to be emperor, for rescue in the north.

Elizabeth poured out her new-found enthusiasm for the cause in a poem called 'Meditation' which she sent to *Blackwood's*. When it was not printed there, she embodied it in the first part of her *Casa Guidi Windows*, which tells the story of the campaigns. From the balcony of their apartment the Brownings had looked down on 12 September, the anniver-

sary of their wedding day, at the crowd passing through the
Piazza Pitti rejoicing at the granting of some constitutional
freedom: the right to a free press and the recruitment of a
national guard of their own to replace the Austrians.

The poem opens with a description of Florence,
emphasizing the richness of works of art to be seen there.
She is moved to some length but also most liveliness by a
description of the statue which the villainous Pietro Borgia
made Michelangelo carve in the snow, laughing from his
palace window as he watched it dissolve. Then she comes to
the crowds shouting '*evviva*' as they marched, laughing and
singing, on that day of liberation:

> ... The day was such a day
> As Florence owes the sun. The sky above,
> Its weight upon the mountains seemed to lay,
> And palpitate in glory, like a dove
> Who has flown too fast, full-hearted – take away
> The image! for the heart of man beat higher
> That day in Florence, flooding all her streets
> And piazzas with a tumult and desire.

She lists the people passing in some sort of ordered procession. 'The Magistracy, with insignia, passed', then lawyers
and priests:

> The Artists; next, the Trades; and after came
> The People – flag and sign, and rights as good, –
> And very loud the shout was for that same
> Motto, 'Il popolo.'

Foreigners bearing their flags joined in. For three hours the
procession went on. 'O heaven, I think that day had noble
use/Among God's days.'

The Austrian archduke, Leopold, brought his children to
the windows of his palace to watch and was greeted with
cheers, the people in their excitement as naïvely over-
confident of his democratic intentions as was Elizabeth
herself.

... I like his face; the forehead's build
Has no capacious genius, yet perhaps
Sufficient comprehension, – mild and sad,
And careful nobly....

And so, God save the Duke, I say with those
Who that day shouted it, and while dukes reign,
May all wear in the visible overflows
Of spirit, such a look of careful pain!
For God must love it better than repose.

The Habsburgs were certainly better known for their out-thrust jaws than for their brains but had withal a tormented air such as the poet falls for here.

A faint element of doubt creeps in:

Meanwhile, in this same Italy we want
Not popular passion, to arise and crush,
But popular conscience, which may covenant
For what it knows. Concede without a blush,
To grant the 'civic guard' is not to grant
The civic spirit....

George Meredith, a younger writer with a deep concern for the cause, summed up the leading Italian personalities who were to emerge in the course of the campaign as the three 'Who blew the breath of life into her frame: Cavour, Mazzini, Garibaldi, these her Brain, her Soul, her Sword.' But at the outset a leader was wanted. Priest or prince? A peasant-fisherman (some symbolism here), in the shape of Garibaldi, was not yet on the horizon, so a chance must be taken on a pope or Louis Napoleon. History was against a ruler-priest but Pius IX might prove an exception.

... We fain would grant the possibility
For *thy* sake, Pio Nono!

Stretch thy feet
In that case – I will kiss them reverently
As any pilgrim to the papal seat!

But Pio Nono's feet were of clay: his failure to support the revolution against the Catholic Austrian state took the heart – and the means – out of it, and he showed personal cowardice in running away from Rome to Gaeta to put himself under the protection of the Bourbon King of Naples, another hated tyrant. Meanwhile in March the Piedmontese king, Charles Albert, was defeated at Novara by Marshal Radetsky and in July Louis Napoleon brought down the newly formed Roman Republic. That same month the Tuscan authorities gave up their resistance and restored the Archduke Leopold as governor.

Elizabeth's disillusion was matched by her indignation. The second part of *Casa Guidi Windows*, written in 1851, accuses the Italians of frivolity and cupidity. Her first enthusiasm for the crowd singing '*evviva*' has turned to cynicism:

> Long live the people! How they lived! and boiled
> And bubbled in the cauldron of the street....
> How down they pulled the Duke's arms everywhere!
> How up they set new café-signs, to show
> Where patriots might sip ices in pure air –
> (The fresh paint smelling somewhat)....

She accused other European governments of cowardice for their non-intervention. England she particularly attacked: the government had done nothing to help any of the 1848 revolts.

> 'Tis treason, stiff with doom, –
> 'Tis gagged despair, and inarticulate wrong,
> Annihilated Poland, stifled Rome,
> Dazed Naples, Hungary fainting 'neath the thong,
> And Austria wearing a smooth olive-leaf
> On her brute forehead, while her hoofs outpress
> The life from these Italian souls, in brief.

In some reviews of the poem when it was published she was rebuked for war-mongering. If she does glorify the taking

up of arms, it was because she felt it was not true pacifism
but business interests that kept England neutral.

> A cry is up in England, which doth ring
> > The hollow world through, that for ends of trade
> And virtue, and God's better worshipping,
> > We henceforth should exalt the name of Peace. . . .

A generation that has known appeasement can understand
her attitude.

Always at her best when writing of an individual experience with which she could identify, she had moving lines on
the death of Garibaldi's Anita on their flight from Rome,
even if it was a far cry from galloping a pony on the Malvern
Hills to mastering a curvetting steed with an infant on the
saddle-bow. When Anita went into battle beside Garibaldi,
Ba-lamb could see herself as an Amazon.

> . . . who, at her husband's side, in scorn,
> > Outfaced the whistling shot and hissing waves,
> > > Until she felt her little babe unborn
> > Recoil, within her, from the violent staves
> > > And bloodhounds of the world, – at which, her life
> > Dropt inwards from her eyes and followed it
> > Beyond the hunters.

This is succeeded by an apologia for the unfortunate
Charles Albert, the Piedmontese king, fated not to die
heroically in battle at Novara but back in Genoa. Nevertheless he was 'shriven in cannon smoke'. It may seem strange
that Elizabeth's main concern with the Crimean War in
which her own country was involved was the fear that
Henrietta's husband might be recalled to the army. She only
associated it with her main interest when she declared the
French had behaved 'magnanimously'.

In 1860 there were to be other poems about the second
phase of the Risorgimento in the volume *Poems before Congress*, notably 'A Tale of Villafranca' and 'A Court Lady'.
The latter poem contains the words:

'Art thou a Lombard, my brother?
Happy art thou,' she cried.

At the end the Court Lady holds the hand of the dying man:

Back he fell while she spoke. She rose to her feet with a spring, –
'That was a Piedmontese! and this is the Court of the King.'

A picture to illustrate this scene was commissioned from
Arthur Hughes by Ellen Heaton in the hope of pleasing
both Elizabeth and Ruskin. It was intended to show a
beautiful young woman in her richest court dress visiting
the wounded in a sordid hospital but Ruskin considered she
was too plainly dressed and that her diamonds did not flash.

# 10

# *Sonnets From The Portuguese*
# 1849–1850

BUT between the two parts of *Casa Guidi Windows* and the hopes aroused and dashed that they recorded, much else had happened to Elizabeth. In spite of other miscarriages since Pisa, on 9 March 1849 she had borne a son, without, it seems, unduly long labour or suffering, for there is nothing about that in the jubilant letters conveying the news to her sisters. She was forty-three but she made a good recovery and the boy was perfectly healthy. He was baptized at the Lutheran Chapel with the names Robert Wiedeman Barrett, later known as 'Penini' or 'Pen'. In letters to Henrietta she envied her having other children for she particularly longed for a girl but she never went her full term again.

In May Browning was very upset on receiving the news of the death of his mother but felt unable to leave wife and child to return home to comfort his father and Sarianna. That summer they got away from the heat of Florence by going to Bagni di Lucca, where most years they had as neighbours the American sculptor William Wetmore Story and his wife. He was of a rich Bostonian family and could have joined his father's law practice but gave this up in order to live in Italy and devote himself to his art. As Henry James put it in a biography with characteristic circumlocution:

The act was a choice, if ever a choice was, with the sense of what he renounced fully mature in him, and with a lively intelligence, though doubtless with some admirably confused ideas – and this is part of the interest of his record – in respect to what he preferred.

Story provided the nearest thing to intellectual companionship for Browning who appreciated his superior knowledge of art as a practitioner and would try his own hand at modelling in the studio. On long walks together they would discuss politics as well as books and pictures, for Story was to be much concerned later with the American war over slavery and deplored what he regarded as English misunderstanding of the issue.

It was at Bagni di Lucca that Elizabeth at last showed Browning her *Sonnets from the Portuguese*, the series of poems she had written at Wimpole Street when he had first declared his love for her. The story goes that she stole up to him as he stood by a window and shyly put the manuscript into his hand.

The title was mischievously chosen to suggest a translation. Elizabeth had intended to call the series *Sonnets from the Bosnian* but Browning said this was meaningless; they must appear to be the poems that Catarina might have written to Camoens in the Portuguese story on which Elizabeth had already published verses. *Fraser's Magazine*, taken in, wrote in its review:

From the Portuguese they may be; but their life and earnestness must prove Mrs. Browning either to be the most perfect of all known translators or to have quickened with her own spirit the framework of another's thought.

The sonnets are some of the most moving love poems in the language and should be read in their entirety as extracts do not do them justice. The woman looks up to her lover – 'The chrism is on thine head, – on mine, the dew, – sees herself unworthy of his love but pours out her heart in gratitude for it – 'What can I give thee back, O liberal/and Princely giver?' – and counts the ways in which she returns it.

How do I love thee? Let me count the ways.
I love thee to the depth and breadth and height
My soul can reach, when feeling out of sight
For the ends of Being and ideal Grace.
I love thee to the level of every day's
Most quiet need, by sun and candlelight.
I love thee freely, as men strive for Right;
I love thee purely, as they turn from Praise;
I love thee with the passion put to use
In my old griefs, and with my childhood's faith;
I love thee with a love I seemed to lose
With my lost saints, – I love thee with the breath,
Smiles, tears, of all my life! – and, if God choose,
I shall but love thee better after death.

The last sonnet ends:

> ... here's eglantine,
> Here's ivy! – take them, as I used to do
> Thy flowers, and keep them where they shall not pine:
> Instruct thine eyes to keep their colours true,
> And tell thy soul, their roots are left in mine.

The theme may seem to be the favourite Victorian one of King Cophetua and the Beggar Maid, the superior Being raising up the inferior to his throne but when Elizabeth and Robert married she was far from a beggar maid. She was much better known and better off, but riches in poetry were all that mattered to either of them. She was no beggar maid in spirit for she had an independent mind and, as we have seen, obedient as she had been to her father she proved capable of the ultimate defiance of his authority. The girl who shocked the Boyds by the way she ignored the conventions of society grew into the woman who ignored the conventions of matrimony; a middle-aged woman in delicate health running away with a penniless man some years her junior who was after her money. In society's terms the Barrett family had a case for being scandalized.

Back in Florence in October Elizabeth was revising the

poems of 1838 and 1844 for a new edition and Browning was working on final drafts of his *Christmas Eve and Easter Day*. A new friend at this time who proved congenial was the American Marchesa d'Ossoli, better known as Margaret Fuller, one of those Brook Farm 'cranks' who always appealed to the Brownings, although in this case her socialism went too far for them. On the night before she was to sail home to America she came to say goodbye. With what Elizabeth called in a letter to Eliza Ogilvy 'her peculiar smile', she had said their ship 'was called Elizabeth and she accepted it as a good omen – though a prediction had been made to her husband that the sea would be fatal to him'. The ship went down in sight of the American shore and she and her husband and child were drowned. For Elizabeth the tragedy recalled to the surface poignant memories never buried very deep.

By 1850 both Brownings were homesick in their different ways. Browning was not cut out to be an expatriate: the lines in 'Home-Thoughts from the Sea' years before were not poetic platitudes:

'Here and here did England help me, – how can I help England?'

He must have missed too the intellectual company he knew in London. For Elizabeth, always less conventional in her outlook, England was the unwelcoming country that greeted Aurora Leigh on her arrival from Italy and that had rejected herself.

> Then, land! – then, England! oh, the frosty cliffs
> Looked cold upon me. Could I find a home ,
> Among those mean red houses through the fog?

But her family sense was strong. She hoped against hope that her father would want to see his grandson, and longed to show Penini to her brothers and to Henrietta – now like herself, disowned since she married – and to Arabel, still living at home and becoming something of a 'do-gooder'. She was also faithful to her old governess, Mrs Orme, and to members of the staff still at Wimpole Street whom she had known since her girlhood.

For Browning, returning to what had been an exceptionally happy home, it was to be sad in a different way, for it would not be the same without his mother. He had, too, a certain sense of guilt that he had not seen her again since leaving England, nor been able to return to help his father and Sarianna.

For both there were personal friends to be seen and a need to assess their position in the literary world, though they would not have put it so baldly. Browning's *Christmas Eve and Easter Day* was due for publication as was a second edition of Elizabeth's *Collected Poems* with the *Sonnets* added.

But in July Elizabeth suffered the worst of her miscarriages, her fourth. For two days she was packed in ice and Robert sat up with her all night. She must have lost a quantity of blood which without transfusions in those days permanently weakened her resistance to lung infections.

During pregnancies she had forgone her drug but how harmless it was to her is shown by the fact that Pen once got hold of it but suffered no ill effects. To return once more to her 'addiction', there was to be a bitter squib from Mrs Julia Ward Howe in an attack on both Brownings in 1857, unworthy of the author of the 'Battle Hymn of the Republic'. Her verses appear to have been written out of pique that they had not acknowledged promptly a copy of her early poems, *Passion Flowers*. It was in *Words for the Hour* that she travestied Browning's title with 'One Word More to E.B.B.'. She dwells on the moral harm from drug-taking, or rather, its unfair influence on poetic inspiration, on those 'who fly with pinions other than their own'.

I shrink before the nameless draught
That helps to such unearthy things,

> And if a drug could lift as high,
> I would not trust its dangerous wings.

Elizabeth took this calmly, writing to Mrs Ogilvy later: 'life is necessary to writing and that I should not be alive except for the help of my morphine.' And she wanted to stay alive: 'I don't want to leave the world while Robert and Wiedeman [Pen] are in it,' and, one might add, with a visit to London, old friends and relations to see and new volumes of their poems to be appraised.

But now in August 1850, they went to Siena for convalescence. At first Elizabeth stopped quietly in the villa they had taken outside the city, but she made so good a recovery that when they moved into Siena itself she was able to accompany Browning to churches and art galleries. He formed several lasting enthusiasms for old masters there, particularly Sodoma. Elizabeth followed his taste but with preferences of her own. Pacchiarotto's 'Virgin and Child' in San Cristofero she would sooner have had than any other picture in Siena, 'if I had leave to carry away what I pleased'. When resting, she turned her hand to embroidering merino frocks for Pen – she who had so loathed needlework as a girl; 'Then one writes & reads a little at intervals . . . and so, life goes on.' She could relax now in a way she had refused to do on doctors' orders years ago at Torquay. What is amazing is the way she survived illnesses and the mental shocks which 'prostrated' her. Delicate physically from a chest weakness, sensitive and highly strung, she was nonetheless no neurotic.

# 11

# First Return Visit to England
# 1851

In the spring of 1851 they felt they were in a position to afford the projected visit to England. They had planned to go first to Rome but, even with the letting of their Casa Guidi apartment, finances would not allow, so they decided instead to see Venice. They set off with Murray's *Handbook* in one hand and Samuel Rogers' travelogue in verse, *Italy*, in the other. They went first by road and then by railway from Mantua, accompanied by the Ogilvys and with Wilson to take care of Pen, now two years old. The child showed a proper sensibility to Venice, 'shrieking with joy at the sight of Saint Mark's', and then turning to embrace Wilson who was carrying him, 'throwing up his arms in delight when he saw the Dogano del Mare'.

Elizabeth was enraptured too by Venice. To Arabel she wrote that for it she would 'give up Florence and twenty Parises'. Not strong enough for much cultural visiting, she was happy to sit in the Piazza San Marco watching Venetian life go by, letting the beauty of the place sink in. Perhaps the better part? She 'liked to receive impressions quietly and deeply without so much talk of this and that', so that, fond as she was of the Ogilvys, it was a relief when they took themselves off elsewhere. David, as well as Browning and Pen, had been ill during the visit so that Elizabeth with her ability to spice gush with acid admitted, 'Venice is as bilious as it is beautiful.'

One adventurous expedition they did make was by steamer to a *fiesta* at Chicoga when they alarmed Wilson by not returning until two in the morning. On another occasion they visited the gardens of the Armenian cemetery and met there an old man who spoke English and claimed to have taught some Armenian to Byron. They also attended the opera several times, for which Elizabeth wrote apologetically to Arabel who might disapprove of theatre-going as a form of what she regarded as luxurious extravagance.

Continuing the journey home, they stopped at Arqua for the sake of Petrarch's little room 'where the great soul exhaled itself'. 'We have great organs of reverence and a taste for old slippers and such gear,' Elizabeth wrote to Eliza Ogilvy. She also told her of Pen's endurance on the tiring journey of sixteen hours by *diligence* from Verona to Milan. He had shown amazing good temper and stamina arriving 'in the highest spirits and the most soup-devouring mood'. The small frame had an unexpected toughness as had his mother when it was called upon, for she managed to climb up the steps to the top of the cathedral at Milan.

Then their route ran through Switzerland and on to Strasbourg, where they found Tennyson and his wife, who were most friendly and, to Elizabeth's delight, showed appreciation of Browning's poetry. Evidently the personal relationship they established was a happy one, for Tennyson offered them the use of his house at Twickenham.

After twenty-four hours of continuous travelling they reached Paris where they would have liked to stay longer, but an appeal came from Arabel not to delay as she had taken rooms for them in Devonshire Street. To choose, on this visit and subsequent ones, to stay so near to Wimpole

Street suggests that the old home was a candle to which Elizabeth was drawn like a moth, to the destruction of her own peace of mind.

In London she missed the easy living conditions of the continent and, anxious as she was to show off Pen to friends and relations, she may have felt it symbolic that before coming over Browning had insisted that she give up putting little embroidered lace caps on Pen's head. These were a fashion for babies and presented to expectant mothers by women friends who had made them, much like matinée jackets today; the boys' had a round cockade at the side and girls' an oval. She had a shiver of apprehension that the boy's father might want the discipline of an English upbringing for him in the future. Would the pretty clothes, which showed off the boy's fair skin and golden curls and were so much admired abroad, be out of place in England and would he feel an exile there, as she was to make the half-Italian Aurora Leigh?

She need not have worried for the relations were properly admiring. Sarianna and Mr Browning received them warmly at New Cross for two days: Henrietta came up from Taunton for a week, and brother George consented to a meeting and afterwards kept up correspondence. Mr Barrett, however, wrote a cruel note of dismissal in reply to his daughter and returned to her unopened all the letters she had written to him. This so poisoned the happiness of the visit that Elizabeth transferred her disappointment to conditions in England in general: climate and domestic life. The welcome of old friends and meeting with new did not make up for the heart-ache caused by her father's attitude, but she put a good face on the social occasions which she saw that Browning so greatly enjoyed. Mr Kenyon, showing signs of age, but kindly and welcoming as ever, gave one of his dinner parties for them, inviting Chorley and Forster and Anna Jameson besides Carlyle, who was already known to Browning. Carlyle greatly impressed Elizabeth who did not find his egotism oppressive. Jane Carlyle later had some of her sharp remarks to make about both of them: Browning she called a 'fluff of feathers', and she did not reciprocate Elizabeth's admiration of her, saying '*she* does not grow on me'.

It was on this visit that Rossetti was brought to call on them by Buchanan Read, a young American travelling in Europe with many introductions. Read was to become celebrated both as a poet and a painter, and his 'Sheridan's Ride' hung above as many nursery bedsteads in the States as did Millais's 'Boyhood of Raleigh' in England. Rossetti had been one of the few to identify the anonymous author of *Pauline* which he had read in the British Museum. He had chanced his luck by writing to Browning to confirm it and, to his great joy, his letter was acknowledged. When they now met, Browning did not disappoint him nor did Elizabeth, though his first impression was of her extreme delicacy – 'so worn out with illness and speaks in the tone of an invalid'. Browning sat to Rossetti for a portrait, but Elizabeth, although putting him off with a polite promise of some other time, told Arabel that she 'refused to be perpetuated in ugliness by the head of the Pre-Raphaelite School'.

Others who called on them in their rooms were Fanny Kemble, divorced from her slave-owner husband, Pierce Butler, and Sara, the youngest daughter of Samuel Taylor Coleridge, married to her cousin, Henry Nelson Coleridge. (She added an appendix to her father's *Aids to Reflection*; 'longer than the work itself', commented Elizabeth.)

The year 1851 was one of excitement in London for the Great Exhibition was held in the Crystal Palace erected in Hyde Park. When Elizabeth heard of the plan for it she wrote critically in *Casa Guidi Windows* that the material progress it celebrated showed disregard for what would now be called the under-privileged, whether individuals or nations.

>                               ...no light
> Of teaching, liberal nations, for the poor,
> Who sit in darkness when it is not night?

Carlyle disapproved too. 'There was confusion enough in the universe,' she heard him growl, 'without building a crystal palace to represent it.' In her letter to Eliza Ogilvy she spells 'crystal' with an 'h', and says she was very tired (and bored?) from visiting the exhibition with Anna Jameson and Robert. She does not appear to have taken Pen who would surely have enjoyed it.

Fearful for Elizabeth's health as autumn approached, they left for Paris on 25 September, Carlyle deciding to travel with them and finding Browning useful as courier to take care of the luggage. 'One of the greatest sights of England,' Elizabeth had called him and the rigours of a Channel crossing did not disillusion her. She even managed to record his pontification about the *mal de mer* from which they all suffered, including Pen and Flush: 'sea-sickness is the most humiliating of the casualties which afflict human nature, except a cold in the head.'

Once settled in rooms on the Champs-Élysées Elizabeth recovered health and spirits and was willing to attend some receptions. Lady Elgin's informal parties, when the hostess herself boiled the kettle for tea and provided bread and butter – unusual at such gatherings – much pleased her, and so did meetings with the eccentric Madame Mohl. A protégée of Madame Récamier, she later became the 'Clarkey' who was one of those to attend Florence Nightingale as secretary-nurse-Cerberus. More important was the beginning of a friendship with the distinguished French critic, Joseph Milsand, who had written appreciatively of Browning in the *Revue des deux Mondes*.

But the invitation that most excited Elizabeth was one from Madame Dudevant, her admired George Sand. For her it was a Royal Command and, despite the coldness of the weather and Robert's lack of enthusiasm, she was determined to accept. 'At last,' she wrote to Miss Mitford, 'I pricked Robert up to the leap, for he was really inclined to sit in his chair and be proud a little. No, said I, you *shant* be proud as I *wont* be proud and we *will* see her. I wont die, if I can help it, without seeing George Sand.' So, muffled up in furs and rugs, she hired a carriage and together they paid their call.

But the visit was not a success. Although it was Mazzini who had provided the introduction and George Sand insisted on kissing Elizabeth cheek to cheek, she did not put herself out for her guests and to the English couple the atmosphere of the salon was not attractive. The sycophantic guests were 'a society of ragged Reds diluted with the lower theatrical' and their ceremonial hand-kissing did not redeem their insufferable habits of smoking and of expectorating into spitoons liberally provided. 'We both tried to please her,' wrote Elizabeth in her disappointment, 'only we felt we could not penetrate – couldn't *touch* her – it was all vain.' Like other feminists, Madame clearly preferred the company of males, for on a later occasion she was seen walking along the Champs-Élysées on Browning's arm and they met again in Italy.

But these months were unfortunate in several ways. Browning's father had got himself entangled with an elderly widow who was suing him for breach of promise; in the court case that followed damages of £800 had somehow to be found and paid. In order to escape from local gossip, Browning arranged for his father and Sarianna to move to Paris where he found them suitable quarters.

Another blow, this time in the literary field, was the discovery that the Shelley letters to which he had written the Introduction for Moxon were forgeries. He had undertaken the work with enthusiasm as it sealed the hero-worship that both he and Elizabeth had shared since youth for the poet, and felt all the more intensely since they had followed so closely in his footsteps in 'the paradise of exiles

– Italy'. Browning had been taken in and had wasted his time.

There was also unpleasantness for Elizabeth when she found that volumes of her poetry were being pirated in the United States. She had many personal friends and admirers among Americans, who rated her higher than did many English critics, and she did not want to join militantly in the complaints that other writers, notably Dickens, were making about the disregard of copyrights and consequent pirating for which there was no redress.

Worse, in December they found that Miss Mitford in her *Recollections* had given an account of the episode of Bro's death. She had been one of the very few people to whom Elizabeth had confided any details and it was a profound shock to find her confidence had not been respected. What she said sounds innocuous enough:

> I have so often been asked what could be the shadow that had passed over that young heart, that, now that time has softened the first agony, it seems to me right that the world should hear the story of an accident in which there was much sorrow, but no blame.

It might have been the suggestion that she had got over her grief (the agony softened) that disturbed Elizabeth – no one likes to hear they have 'got over' a tragedy. Miss Mitford was apologetic but clearly felt that it was all so long ago and so much had happened since that Elizabeth was over-reacting. Their friendship by correspondence survived, as it had survived the shock of Elizabeth's marriage, and with most of the old warmth but from now on there were to be other women who formed close friendships with Elizabeth to each other's resentment and not always to Elizabeth's comfort.

# 12

# Interest in the Paranormal
# 1852

A VISIT to London was now part of the Brownings' yearly plans, undertaken from Elizabeth's point of view out of family loyalty to Arabel (with whom she can have had little in common) and nostalgic affection for old friends like John Kenyon who had been good to her and to Robert. But the main reason was to satisfy what she must have seen as Browning's desire for the society of his peers.

In July 1852 they travelled once again from Paris and stayed at 58 Welbeck Street, as before in the Wimpole Street neighbourhood. On this visit, among the celebrities they met for the first time were Ruskin and Charles Kingsley. Ruskin had referred to Elizabeth's 'spirituality' in the first volume of *Stones of Venice* and was throughout her life a warm admirer, even when in his mildly teasing way he objected to her excessive use of Greek which he could not understand, and, as late as *Aurora Leigh*, her made-up compounds; he complained that he could not find 'phalanstery' in Johnson's *Dictionary* and that 'dynastick' hurt him like a stick. When they lunched with Ruskin and his wife, Effie, in Denmark Hill, where they were then living with Ruskin's parents, Elizabeth liked Ruskin personally as much as she had always admired his writings, though she found Effie 'pretty and elegant but incapable of intelligent effort', in fact, frivolous. No doubt she was at her worst in the frustrating atmosphere of her in-laws' household.

Charles Kingsley, exponent of an anti-papistical, muscular Christianity congenial to Browning, she found impressive but not *sympathique*, and would have found him less so could she have foreseen what he was to say about the spiritualism in which she was to become involved. When he attacked with his usual forcefulness, a 'mesmerising, table-turning, spirit-raising, spiritualising, Romanising generation', he brought in also, somewhat irrelevantly, those who were admirers of Shelley. Which was worse to his mind, atheism or the Papacy?

A very pleasant event was the Tennysons' invitation to the christening of their son, Hallam. At the last minute Elizabeth was not well enough to attend but Browning enjoyed the occasion and distinguished himself by tossing the baby up in his arms to the infant's chuckling delight so that Tennyson exclaimed: 'Ah, that's as good as a glass of champagne to him.'

Christenings with parties to follow for friends as well as relations and godparents seem to have been the fashion, for the Brownings together went to one at the Monckton Milnes' which Elizabeth described to Miss Mitford: 'Monckton Milnes had a brilliant christening luncheon and his baby was made to sweep in [in] India muslin and Brussels lace among a circle of admiring guests.' Pen had behaved like an angel, she insisted, though he disgraced her by refusing to kiss the baby.

Less happy had been an expedition in July to Ealing to the house of some people called Rymer who were willing hosts to 'believers' and able to introduce them to Daniel Douglas Home, a celebrated (some would say notorious) medium. The Brownings had heard of him in Florence through other interested friends, though Sophia Cottrell had been there when in London and was not impressed. The party sat in a darkened room round a table on which lay a wreath of clematis. They waited in expectant silence until the wreath was seen to move and then arrive on Elizabeth's head. The believers were thrilled that spirit hands had so directed the flowers (opportunely gathered that afternoon from the garden by the Rymer children), but Browning insisted that the 'spirit hands' were attached to the feet of the medium who manipulated the wreath. It was no more than the sort of trick a good conjuror might perform. He said nothing but no doubt showed his disgust and disapproval. He did not want his wife to be made a fool of. Later Browning asked for a repeat of the seance when he would bring an independent witness, Helen Faucit, but the Rymers made some excuse to refuse. Home had the audacity to call at Welbeck Street, but the comments of his unwilling host caused him to take a hasty leave. Browning's attitude was summed up in no uncertain terms in a third-person letter written in answer to an unknown couple who had asked for his considered opinion on 'table-rapping'. Elizabeth added to the letter: 'I enclose to you in his handwriting an account of the impressions he received. Mine, I must frankly say, were entirely different.'

On this whole question of 'table-rapping', as it was currently called, it must be remembered that it was a fashion imported from America and 'fashion' is a word to be used advisedly. It can be dated exactly as starting in 1848 when two girls in Hydesville, New York, claimed to be intermediaries, 'mediums', between the living and the dead. The method they employed to get in touch was through 'percussion sounds', that is, knocking or rapping on tables.

This 'spiritualism' was a development from the earlier cult of 'magnetic sleep' or mesmerism, and grew into movements of the furniture itself, automatic writing, levitation and other paranormal phenomena. It had a revival in the 1920s when, very naturally, those who had been bereaved in the 1914–18 war hoped to get in touch with the dead.

Elizabeth's other enthusiasm, for Louis Napoleon, was encouraged by Landor whom she liked much better this time when they met again at Mr Kenyon's, for he was on her side in defiant support of Louis Napoleon. He had known him during his exile in London and considered him 'a man of wonderful genius'. It was a particular joy to Elizabeth that on their return to Paris in October they were able to witness one of Louis Napoleon's 'progresses', rehearsals for the later entry as emperor. Some friends, the Corkrans (Fraser Corkran was Paris correspondent of the *Morning Chronicle*), invited them to their house in the Boulevard des Italiens to view the procession from a balcony overlooking the street. Pen, as excited as his mother, waved his black velvet hat with the feather in it, but Browning, suspicious of any dictator, however much of a liberator he claimed to be, was less enthusiastic.

A week later they went on to Florence, having to rent a private carriage for the crossing of Mont Cenis as the height brought on pains in Elizabeth's chest. Elizabeth was happy to be home again, and their rooms at Casa Guidi were none the worse for the wear and tear of the tenants. She set about a regular routine of lessons for Pen but she was insistent in letters to Henrietta against pushing him. He wanted to read and write, she declared, because he saw his parents at it. She may not have considered it to be pushing him but he was over-stimulated by the subjects she covered, besides his father's piano lessons, and over-exposed to flattery for his looks and manners which were certainly charming.

To Browning Florence was dull after London, especially since his play *Colombe's Birthday* was to be put on at the Haymarket Theatre in April 1853. With this forthcoming production he felt more able to hold his own with writers he knew or might meet in England.

Even if he felt no resentment at being considered so

utterly his wife's consort in Florence, he naturally warmed to the enthusiastic admiration felt towards him by a newly appointed young attaché, Robert Lytton, son of the famous novelist, Edward Bulwer-Lytton. Lytton longed to devote himself to writing but met with no encouragement. His father wanted him to make a success of a diplomatic career and somehow earn – or marry – enough money to keep up the vast mansion of Knebworth in Hertfordshire that he would inherit. The difference of opinion was settled in a way that looks satisfactory to both sides but was really a heart-break to young Robert. His father consented to help get his work published in England if he would adopt a pseudonym. 'Owen Meredith' was decided upon (which led to complications later with George Meredith) and Lytton went on to a successful career ending up, reluctantly, as Viceroy of India.

His poems are mostly remembered now for the frequency of their appearance in that anthology of bad verse, *The Stuffed Owl*. He is at times a master of bathos and has a poor ear for the foot in scansion. One set of verses called 'Going Back Again' ends:

> She sat with her guitar on her knee,
>     But she was not singing a note,
> For someone had drawn (ah, who could it be?)
>     A knife across her throat.

(A 'zither' would have been a better musical instrument for scansion.) Tennyson had been just as bad in his first version of the death of Iphigenia in 'A Dream of Fair Women':

> One drew a sharp knife, thro' my tender throat
>     Slowly and nothing more.

When John Lockhart unkindly asked what more she wanted, Tennyson changed the lines to the memorable:

> The bright death quivered at the victim's throat
>     Touched: and I knew no more.

Perhaps genius can have second thoughts impossible to talent.

A poem of Lytton's dedicated to Browning calls him one 'who dwells among the Appenine and there has strung a harp of Anakim', an allusion of Browningesque obscurity. But he does succeed in evoking with some charm the emotions that Italy stirred in the hearts of Anglo-Saxons in the mid-Victorian era.

> Midnight, and love, and youth, and Italy!
>> Love in the land where love most lovely seems!
> Land of my love, tho' I be far from thee,
>> Lend, for love's sake, the light of those moonbeams.
> The spirit of thy cypress-groves and all
>> Thy dark-eyed beauty for a little while
>> To my desire....

It is a pity he did not turn more often to intentional comedy like this extract from Murray's *Guide* that he turned into verse:

> At Coblentz a bridge of boats crosses the Rhine
> And from thence the road, winding by Ehrenbreitstein
> Passes over the frontier of Naasau.
>> ('N.B.
> No custom house here since the Zollverein'.
>> See Murray, paragraph 30).

In spite of his admiration, he found Browning rather overpowering; but he adored Elizabeth and she in turn became a mother-figure to him as woman and as author. He had known little affection as a child, caught between his parents' hate for each other. This and disappointments in love and in literary hopes had made him shy and withdrawn but at Casa Guidi he came out. A slim and handsome melancholy youth, lovelorn withal, naturally appealed to Elizabeth and she devoted a lot of time to him. Her influence brought to the surface an innate charm of manner that was to make him popular in embassies all over Europe, and she encouraged him to persist with his writing. His epic, *Clytemnestra*, received from the *Athenaeum* the same advice it had given Elizabeth for her *Prometheus Bound*, which was to keep off Aeschylus. But with his *Lucille*, a novel in verse of the type of *Aurora Leigh*, he enjoyed considerable success during his appointments in Vienna and Paris.

When Bulwer-Lytton himself came out, Elizabeth could forgive him for being the dandy he was considered in London and for his neglect of his son when she found he was sympathetic on the subject of table-rapping. He was so deeply interested in all psychical phenomena that he has been claimed as a member of the secret Rosicrucian Society. His novels with occult themes enjoyed a popularity comparable to science fiction today.

During this autumn and winter in Florence Elizabeth's interest in spiritualism intensified: an obsession that her husband could not share. In a sense they were each as irrational and prejudiced as the other. She was too credulous and he was too sceptical. In Browning's case, he was unduly influenced by his distaste for the sort of people who professed paranormal powers, forcibly expressed later in 'Mr. Sludge, the Medium'. Elizabeth, he considered, was too much of an angel to be suspicious, though Sophia Cottrell came to share his feeling of disquiet at the integrity of those who professed mediumistic powers. Home, for instance, she wrote in her *Memoir*, was a 'man of no high principle and would, if he could not obtain the information he wished by the communication of the spirit, not scruple to cheat'. She also noted the triviality of the information communicated.

Elizabeth was troubled by this but hoped that some psychic phenomena were true. In a curious way she felt that communication with 'the other side' would enhance her knowledge of life and enable her to 'write better and stronger'.

Browning put up with differences of opinion which did not get in the way of more important things in their life together. The thing he hated most was apathy or indifference. 'Accidie' to him was the deadliest of the seven sins; better a wrong opinion than none. As ever, Elizabeth puts it best herself: 'I can conceive of a strong attachment recovering from the shock of unexpected points of difference and of two souls growing together again after all.' Poets the Brownings might be who had made a romantic marriage but it was not the fabulous happy ending of some fairy tale. There was everyday life to be lived and adjustments to make as for any other couple. What is remarkable is that two people of such determined characters made them so well.

There is no reason to doubt her sincerity and its continuance for the rest of her life when Elizabeth wrote to Henrietta in March 1853: 'May you be happier and happier. Here am I in the seventh year of marriage, happier than on the seventh day. The love not only stays but grows, thank God for it.' 'Grow' is the operative word: it is a relationship which does not develop that rots and dies.

Elizabeth mellowed in that she became less wilful than the girl at Hope End and there are no records of bad temper but at the same time she kept her innocence. Her enthusiasms were as naïve as her intellectual ability was strong; this irritated Henry James but Browning thought it angelic. In marriage she was prepared for give and take, and this was specially noticeable in her ceasing to claim selfish rights to exclusiveness. Her former refusals to meet people became considerably modified, not only in deference to her husband's enjoyment of society but also in recognition of an element of pretentiousness and vanity in previous withdrawals. The many and varied names of their visitors show how accessible their home became. In fact, Elizabeth came to 'tolerate an acquaintance' sometimes too indiscriminately, as the names of callers, particularly the literary ladies, show.

# 13

# In Rome and Florence
## 1853–1854

At last, in November 1853, the Brownings achieved Rome, their visit having been put off several times before. They took eight days over the journey by *vettura*, stopping at Assisi for the sake of St Francis and at Terni to see the Velino waterfall.

The Storys had gone ahead by the sea route from Leghorn to engage rooms and the two families met in high spirits, but on the very evening of the Brownings' arrival, the Story's son, Joe, became ill and died before morning. The daughter, Edith, for fear of infection was taken in by the Page family in the apartment below the Brownings. She also became ill as did the Pages' child but mercifully both recovered.

Elizabeth was frantic at the risk for Penini but felt she could not run away with him and leave the Storys to their grief with possibly worse to come. 'Rome is spoiled for me,' she wrote, after accompanying Mrs Story to the child's grave in the Protestant Cemetery where, as she well knew, the Shelleys' son, Wilmouse, had been laid some thirty years before.

But she and Robert made themselves go out and about, not only sightseeing but also visiting the studios of artists working in the city. The young and handsome Frederic Leighton was there, finishing the monumental picture that was to secure his early and lasting fame, 'Cimabue's Madonna carried in procession in Florence'; Thackeray, who modelled Clive Newcome on him, told Millais that he would have to look to his laurels with this young rival on the scene. Others, English and American, celebrated at the time but forgotten since, were Thomas Crawford (father of the novelist, Marion Crawford), who had fought with the Italians; John Gibson, who enjoyed a brief resurgence of recognition when his 'Tinted Venus' came up for sale in the 1960s; William Fisher to whom Browning sat for a portrait in which appears the first streak of grey in his beard.

He also sat to William Page, called the 'American Titian', who favoured a special technique by which he insisted the paint he used would never fade or darken. Browning, always interested in the methods of a painter's work, wrote to tell Rossetti that nevertheless the portrait quickly deteriorated, quoting: 'Kings do not die – they only fade away.' The Brownings thought Page worthy of an introduction to Ruskin when he went over to England. Elizabeth wrote:

He is an earnest, simple, noble artist & man, – who carries his Christianity down from his deep heart to the point of his brush. Draw him out to talk to you & you will find it worth while. He has learnt much from Swedenborg, & used it in his views upon art. Much of it (if new) may sound to you wild and dreaming but the dream will admit of logical inference & philosophical induction, and, when you open your eyes, it is still there.

Of the nude picture refused by the Salon but without bringing him either reputation or notoriety, she wrote: 'See what a wonder of light & colour & space & breath-taking air, he put into his "Venus rising from the sea". . . . refused on the grounds of nudity this summer.'

There was also a young American sculptor, Hatty

Hosmer, who had sold her 'Sleeping Fawn' for the surprisingly large sum of £1000. She was so far liberated that she insisted on walking about the streets of Rome alone and, even more shocking, riding her horse without an escort, a practice that had to be stopped because of the near-riots it caused. The Brownings thoroughly enjoyed her high spirits: Elizabeth always sympathetic to a woman who showed courage and independence.

They also enjoyed the company of Fanny Kemble, 'resting' from the theatre. She could tell first-hand stories of the slavery she had witnessed on her former husband's plantations. What Elizabeth had written in her 'Runaway Slave' was no exaggeration.

Fanny's sister, Adelaide Sartoris, once a prima donna, was now content to be famous for her receptions. These were always attended by Frederic Leighton for, still handsome at thirty-five to his twenty-five, Adelaide was an admirable *femme de trente ans* for his education – not that this included any sexual initiations. Mr Sartoris might be conveniently off stage but she was never unfaithful to him in the marital sense. While Elizabeth's protégé went on to become a viceroy, Adelaide's was the first painter to be made a peer.

Of such company, Fanny wrote: 'Thackeray is here and the Brownings so it is not our fault if we are not both witty and poetical.' Anny, aged sixteen, the elder of Thackeray's two daughters, described Fanny's belief in a regular routine which led her to wear her dresses in rotation regardless of the circumstances. One quiet evening in the Via Bocca di Leone when the room was lit only by a couple of candles and Mrs Browning was sitting over a wood fire 'in her dusky gown unrelieved', Fanny entered in most unsuitable stately crimson, edged with gold. It was the day for the red dress.

Together with Hatty and Leighton and the French scholar Jean-Jacques Ampère (son of the scientist who gave his name to electrical current), they would go for picnics among the ruins, 'the site once of a city great and gay', or out on the Campagna. In the evenings, when Browning went on his own to dinners or soirées – 'as a sort of lion,' Elizabeth wrote, 'he has his range in society' – she would let Anny and Harriet (Minny) Thackeray keep her company.

With Thackeray himself Elizabeth was never quite at ease although she appreciated the well-informed articles on the Italian situation which he put in the *Cornhill*. He had been contemporary with Bro at Charterhouse and she may have been nervous in case he should refer to this. Also he had a certain boisterousness like Landor which she found distasteful, though it made him a great success with Pen as with other children. She was however too professional as a writer to bear him any ill-will when he rejected her poem, 'Lord Walter's Wife', on the grounds that the *Cornhill* was a 'family' magazine: 'There are things *my* squeamish public will not hear on Monday, though on Sundays they listen to them without scruple.' The poem is highly moral as the wife rejects the seducer but it was probably the term 'harlot' in the last verse but two which was open to objection.

But the parties and the friendships were as nothing to the apprehension both parents felt when they saw Penini less lively and looking off-colour. The Roman spring bred fatal fevers, as tragically the Shelleys had found, so they made plans to leave and returned to Florence at the end of May.

Home again Penini recovered and his parents settled into a more regular routine than had been possible in Rome. The mornings were reserved for work; lessons for Penini and composition for his parents. Elizabeth had 'broken the back' of *Aurora Leigh* at 30–40 lines a day but still had a long way to go, and Robert had to 'set his poetical house in order' for the publication of *Men and Women*.

Till June 1855 they remained in Florence without visits to cooler climates for the summer or excursions elsewhere. Elizabeth's friendship with Isa Blagden developed at this time. A pleasing personality of great kindliness, she was author of a novel or two but did not claim any prescriptive right to the Brownings' company on this count. She gathered together the expatriate lame dogs and poor relations of the famous at her 'tea parties with a sunset to correspond' in her villa on Bellosguardo. Elizabeth wrote that she could walk home with Robert 'by moonlight, or starlight at worst, through that exquisite avenue of grand cypresses half a mile long'; and again in *Aurora Leigh*:

> 'Tis a tower which keeps
> A post of double-observation o'er
> The valley of Arno (holding as a hand
> The outspread city) straight toward Fiesole
> And Mount Morello and the setting sun. . . .

Women writers often surround themselves with a court or a supporting chorus. Women are as prone as artists of the male sex to homosexual tendencies although more often kept latent. Evidently lesbianism was recognized by Elizabeth and amused rather than shocked her for she writes both to Sarianna (with whom she was not really on intimate terms) and to Isa about the joining 'in holy matrimony' of Ellen Heaton and Fanny Haworth. The pooling of their incomes would be an advantage for their social climbing – 'glory of all kinds is increased'. She goes further to Isa, referring to Ellen as 'Monsieur le Mari'.

Elizabeth, with husband and son and work to do of major significance, kept clear of emotional involvement; 'not drawn into love' with women who sought reflected glory, like satellites from her sun, except in the case of Sophia Eckley where she was to go from extremes of affection to utter repudiation. It was the women who became emotional in jealousy of each other, only united in dislike of Sophia, who was in particular enmity with Ellen Heaton, competing for the honour of providing a portrait of Elizabeth that was to be the first and unique. Ellen still forced her way in as she had long ago in Wimpole Street. Elizabeth described it to Arabel: when, in Rome, Azeglio* came, Robert told Ferdinando to admit no one else. Other callers went away but Miss Heaton returned after a short interval. 'Who was Azeglio? (she didn't know of course – not she!) but where could she see him? In what street did he live? To what church did he go?'

Another character they were bound to meet was Seymour Kirkup, made a *barone* for his discovery of the portrait of Dante by Giotto. A survivor of times past, he had known the Rossettis' father as a patriot rebel and had attended with Trelawny the burial of Shelley's ashes in Rome. Browning might have warmed to him for these touches of 'eagle's feather', but Kirkup's fanaticism over spiritualism put him off. A convinced spiritualist, he was hardly a convincing one.

Their most distinguished visitor during the year was Charles Eliot Norton from Boston. He was an American Mr Kenyon on a grander scale for there are few eminent Victorians with whom he did not correspond. He knew 'everyone' but it is difficult to find how well they knew him as there are few records of what he was like or how he lived, beyond the fact that he was the first Professor of Fine Art at Harvard.

Very different was Brinsley Norton, son of the famous Caroline. He had married a peasant girl and settled with her in Florence – just the sort of romantic figure that Elizabeth admired.

In the same villa lived Frederick Tennyson and his wife. With no chance of rivalling his younger brother as a poet, he was a contented music-lover and organized frequent concerts in the large salon of the Villa Torrigiani. He tried some table-rapping but said sardonically of Elizabeth's enthusiasm that she was 'never so happy as when she can

* Marquis d'Azeglio, a leader of the Moderate Reform Party in 1848 whose political tract, *I Casi di Romagna*, was widely circulated in 1846.

get into the thick of mysterious Clairvoyants, Rappists, Ecstatics and Swedenborgians'.

One event to sadden Elizabeth, a link with her old life gone, was the death of Flush from no accident but that of old age.

In April she began to ask Henrietta how bonnets were being worn in England, whether 'dropping off behind', and complained that Robert's interest in her clothes meant that she would have to wear hats 'like other people'. He was a tyrant in this. For the sake of the Empress Eugénie, who made crinolines fashionable, Elizabeth took to one and liked the coolness it provided; presumably fewer petticoats had to be worn underneath.

They left for London in June by ship from Leghorn to Marseilles. At Lyons there was a contretemps that for Elizabeth would have amounted to tragedy but for its happy ending: one of their boxes was missing. Distraught, she wrote to her brother, Alfred, whom she had found unexpectedly in Marseilles planning to marry a Barrett cousin, Lizzie, at one time housed as a poor relation in Wimpole Street. As he was described on his passport as being 'on her Majesty's service' he may have been in a position to make official enquiries.

Will you help us? We have lost a box – a square deal box with a black top – it is locked & contains hats, collars, lace, etc.

Only in a postscript does she add that it contained about ten pounds worth of things, 'besides MS notes to a book'. The MS was of *Aurora Leigh*. Happily the box was recovered, complete with Pen's finery, so much more important than her manuscript.

They stopped in Paris in order to see Mr Browning and Sarianna. Here they were disconcerted by the discovery that Wilson was pregnant by Ferdinando Romagnoli. They had no reason to distrust him as a servant and respected him for having been a freedom fighter. Less shocked than most middle-class couples at what had happened, they did not dismiss such useful attendants but saw to it that they were married at the British consulate, as the unorthodox Shelleys had seen to it that their Paolo married Elise. Elizabeth's main worry was that Wilson would no longer be sleeping in the same room as Pen and from now on he shared his mother's room. The day after the wedding, 11 July 1855, they crossed to England.

# 14

# Publication of *Aurora Leigh*
# 1856

THEY reached London at 3 a.m. and went to rooms at 13 Dorset Street, again close to Wimpole Street. Elizabeth went there most days with Pen, carefully between the hours of 10 a.m. and 4 p.m. when Mr Barrett would be out. Once she left Pen with one of his uncles and they were romping in the hall when Mr Barrett appeared. 'Whose child is that?' he asked. 'Ba's.' On receiving that reply he went into his room without a further word.

There was an evening of delight for the Rossetti brothers when they were invited to Dorset Street to hear Tennyson reading his *Maud*. Rossetti sat in a corner quietly sketching the Laureate but critical of his complaints about the notices the poem had received. 'His conversation was really one perpetual groan,' he wrote to William Allingham. 'All this to the intense wonder of Browning, who, as you know, treats reviewers in the way they deserve.' Elizabeth also commented on the evening to Arabel: 'He [Tennyson] opened his heart to us (and the second bottle of port) and interrupted his reading to exclaim, "There's a wonderful touch; that's very tender" – and it was.'

After their departure Rossetti wrote again to Allingham:

The Brownings are long gone back now and with them one of my delights – an evening resort where I never feel unhappy. How large a part of the real world, I wonder, are those two small people? Taking meanwhile so little room in any railway carriage and hardly needing a double bed at the Inn.

In November when the Brownings were in Paris for another autumnal stay, Rossetti was also there and visited them several times. He went round the Louvre with Browning whose knowledge of the pictures and their painters enormously impressed him: 'encyclopaedically beyond that of Ruskin himself'. When they were in London the next year, Rossetti, always generous with his friends, brought Edward Burne-Jones to call and again in 1859 gave him an introduction when he was going out to Italy with Val Prinsep. Rossetti also took charge of Browning's portrait by William Page (much as he disliked it) and saw to its framing and despatch to the Royal Academy.

The end of the friendship is a sad one.* Browning had sent Rossetti each of his books as they came out and received sincerely grateful letters in reply. In 1872 when *Fifine at the Fair* arrived, Rossetti wrote: 'Thanks once more for a new book bearing your name loved as of old. And even before I read it, let me say, thanks. . . .' When he did open it, evidently leafing through from the back, he took it that the picture of the remorseful bridegroom was modelled on himself and his grief over Lizzie's death. Browning had not intended this but Rossetti, then in a state of paranoia, was bitterly hurt. On Rossetti's death, Browning regretted the break with him and was one of the subscribers to the memorial by Madox Brown in Cheyne Gardens, Chelsea.

The year 1855 was memorable for the publication of Browning's *Men and Women* in which first appeared most of his best-known poems, among them 'Andrea del Sarto' whose pictures Elizabeth could now see in the original. The 'epilogue' was his dedication to Elizabeth under the some-

* For more see article in *Princeton University Library Chronicle* (1972).

what misleading title of 'One Word More' as it contained twenty stanzas.

> There they are, my fifty men and women
> Naming me the fifty poems finished!
> Take them, Love, the book and me together:
> Where the heart lies, let the brain lie also.

The theme of the poem is the desire of a painter, Raphael, to express his love in words, and of a poet, Dante, to express himself in paint. Stanza xx ends:

> Oh, their Rafael of the dear Madonnas,
> Oh, their Dante of the dread Inferno,
> Wrote one song – and in my brain I sing it,
> Drew one angel – borne, see, on my bosom!

One of Rossetti's earliest pictures was on this same subject. It shows Dante interrupted by 'certain persons of importance' as he tries to draw a picture of Beatrice on the anniversary of her death. There is another link with the Pre-Raphaelites in that one of the few favourable reviews of *Men and Women* was an enthusiastic one in the *Oxford and Cambridge Magazine* from William Morris, then an undergraduate at Exeter College.

The volume received mostly adverse notices when it received any at all. The *Athenaeum* grieved over 'energy wasted and power mis-spent – fancies chaste and noble, overhung by the "seven veils" of obscurity'. For once Browning allowed himself to harbour some bitterness which Elizabeth expressed more openly in disgust at the 'blindness, deafness and stupidity' of critics and public.

They crossed to Paris in October and were there for the rejoicings in February 1856, when a son was born to Napoleon III and Empress Eugénie. Browning so far met Elizabeth's enthusiasm as to consent to go out and watch the celebrations of the heir's baptism though his poem on the occasion, 'Apparent Failure', concentrates more on his visit

to the morgue in which he conjectures what had been the
life stories of the bodies exposed there; a subject for 'men
and women'. His chauvinism comes out in the lines where
he is not to be deterred from entering.

> I plucked up heart and entered, – stalked,
> Keeping a tolerable face
> Compared with some whose cheeks were chalked:
> Let them! No Briton's to be baulked.

In June they were in London again, accepting John
Kenyon's offer of his house in Devonshire Place as he was in
bad health and had been ordered to the Isle of Wight by his
doctors. There they visited him and stayed on at Ventnor, to
which place Mr Barrett had exiled his family on hearing the
Brownings were to be in London. Elizabeth was ready to
risk these confrontations, always hoping her father would
soften towards her. When this did not happen, she was
consoled by the attentions that Pen received from his Aunt
Arabel and adoring uncles. They also went to stay at Taunton with Henrietta and, on a brief return to London, appropriately in his own home, Elizabeth dedicated to Kenyon
what she regarded as her most important work, *Aurora
Leigh*:

> Through my various efforts in literature and steps in life, you
> have believed in me, borne with me, and have been generous to
> me, far beyond the common uses of mere relationship or sym-
> pathy of mind.

He was able to see this and appreciate it before his death
which they heard about when they were back home in
December 1856. His generosity to them in his life was
perpetuated by the large legacies he left to each in his will.

*Aurora Leigh* received a hostile reception from most of the
reviewers, certainly from all the influential ones; the more
respectable the worse. Only the *Globe*, the *Daily News* and
the *Literary Gazette* praised it, the latter ranking the author

with the Hebrew prophets, Milton and Jeremy Taylor. George Barrett declared to Arabel that it was worse than *Don Juan*, agreeing with the *Dublin University Magazine* that it was 'a pity the authoress had written a book which is almost a closed volume for her own sex'. There were reports that amused the author of its being read by many girls in society under the bedclothes.

The verse which referred to 'breasts' and 'paps' was particularly shocking as the *National Review* pointed out while quoting it:

> Never flinch,
> But still, unscrupulously epic, catch
> Upon the burning lava of a song
> The full-veined, heaving, double-breasted Age:
> That, when the next shall come, the men of that
> May touch the impress with reverent hand, and say
> 'Behold, – behold the paps we all have sucked!'

But the public bought it: the first edition was quickly sold out and the lending libraries rationed their subscribers to two days each. Demand continued, so that in June 1860 there had to be a fifth edition.

The young progressives in art and literature adored it; the Rossettis were enthusiastic and Swinburne wrote: 'the advent of "Aurora Leigh" can never be forgotten by any lover of poetry who was old enough at the time to read it . . . it is one of the longest poems in the world and there is not a dead line in it.' Ruskin, doyen of the *avant-garde*, told Browning that he considered it 'the greatest poem in the English language and the first perfect poetical expression of the Age'. This was echoed by Robert Lytton who called it 'the perfectly successful expression of a whole civilisation'. Old Leigh Hunt, a leading rebel in his time, also wrote to Browning 'of this unique, wonderful and immortal poem with its astonishing admixture of masculine power and feminine tenderness'.

The best known of hostile critics posthumously is Edward Fitzgerald who wrote: 'Mrs Browning's death is rather a relief to me, I must say: no more *Aurora Leighs*, thank God.' This elicited Browning's violent hate poem in reply dashed off impetuously and sent to the *Athenaeum*:

> I chanced upon a new book yesterday:
> I opened it, and, where my finger lay
> 'Twixt page and uncut page, these words I read
> – Some six or seven at most – and learned thereby
> That you, Fitzgerald, whom by ear and eye
> She never knew, 'thanked God my wife was dead.'
> Ay, dead! and were yourself alive, good Fitz,
> How to return you thanks would task my wits:
> Kicking you seems the common lot of curs –
> While more appropriate greeting lends you grace:
> Surely to spit there glorifies your face –
> Spitting from lips once sanctified by Hers.

To be fair, Fitzgerald's remark was in a private letter which escaped the censoring eye of an editor years later in 1889 and Browning only came upon it by unlucky chance. It was a literary not a personal judgment and based on his prejudice against women writers, for he went on: 'A woman of great genius, I know: but what is the upshot of it all? She and her sex had better mind the kitchen and their children and, perhaps, the Poor.'

In 1857 Fitzgerald was amomg the few admirers of *Casa Guidi Windows* saying, 'it preserves the charm of impulse and *go*, not added and altered many times till all is ripe and rotten.' He even said that it made its author 'a greater poet than Tennyson' but it would not be lasting, for to him women's art had a built-in obsolescence. In a different field he shook his head over Jane Austen because 'she never went out of the Parlour' (regardless of the fact that a parlour can be a *huis clos* holding all hell).

It is bound to be conjectured how far *Aurora Leigh** is

---

* For a review of *Aurora Leigh*, narrative and themes, see Appendix II, p. 131.

autobiographical – to which it may be replied, 'Not at all.' Elizabeth makes use of her personal experience in descriptions of places or scenes but it is far from being an author's wish-fulfilment or self-indulgent confession. It is more a paean of thanksgiving that her own way had been so much less hard than her heroine's – 'there but for the grace of God go I.' For Elizabeth there had been a loving home in childhood and no hard struggle for fame.

Aurora's obstinacy and self-righteousness makes her an unsympathetic heroine; perhaps in this there is something of her author's own determination, a quality she felt she needed to encourage in herself. Elizabeth lets herself go in acid criticism of society, literary and fashionable. In this she is not attacking something of which she felt deprived and was therefore jealous, for she was always able to choose her own friends as she had chosen her career and, indeed, her husband. The boredom she suffered as a girl in paying those polite afternoon calls with Aunt Bummy must have gone deep to foster so much indignation and bitterness.

It is to be remembered that at the time despondent isolation was expected of poets. Goethe with his *Werther* and, nearer home, Byron, had made melancholy *de rigueur*, as Wordsworth had made love of Nature and solitude, so that there would not seem to contemporaries the artistic self-righteousness that a later generation finds in lines like,

> Sometimes
> Impatient of some crowded room's closed smell
> You throw a window open and lean out
> To breathe a long breath in the dewy night
> And cool your angry forehead.

Writers and artists were not expected to be good mixers.

The poem may be, has been, claimed as a feminist epic, a manifesto for women's rights. It is this in an individual sense but not in general. Aurora sets out to gain an independent living by her pen and succeeds, but this is by personal effort not by winning political rights or privileges. She is indignant at the cruel treatment Marian receives from her parents as a child and angry at the duplicity of Lady Waldemar's maid and the callous indifference of that lady herself who did not take trouble to find out to what fate she was consigning Marian. She is horrified to hear of conditions at the brothel but there is no suggestion that a way to save the victims would be through such things as Romney's bills or the rescue homes in which her own sister Arabel was involved. Regeneration must come from inside, from the spirit not from legislation. In this Elizabeth underrates her own influence for her 'Cry of the Children' was a piece of propaganda that helped on the crusade for the Factory Acts, and in the fight for Italian liberation she was an activist.

Feminine and political aspiration aside, *Aurora Leigh* from the literary point of view has qualities that are lasting and the wheat in it is worth winnowing from the chaff.

## 15

# Impressions of the Brownings and Penini 1857–1858

An impression of the Brownings as they appeared in these years is provided by Mrs Kinney, wife of the American ambassador to the court of King Victor Emmanuel. Like the other literary dabblers, Elizabeth Clementine had had some poems and articles published. She married William Kinney when he was owner of the *Newark New Jersey Daily Advertiser* and professed herself both bored and shocked by the society into which his official duties had plunged her. She was glad to escape from Turin to Florence where she 'could choose friends from the congenial few'.

First impressions of the Brownings were unpromising. 'First I was disappointed in their looks,' wrote Mrs Kinney in her *Memoir*. 'Mrs. Browning appeared many years older than her husband, though in fact she was only five', and this was accentuated by the way 'she wore her abundant black hair, straight down from the crown of her head on each side of rather high cheek bones where it was to begin curling in a sort of large, loose fashion of its own.' She considered Elizabeth would have appeared 'much younger and better looking had her hair been dressed somewhat back from her face'. Browning she found the very opposite of his wife: 'rather below medium height but broad shouldered with a round head, too large for his body, set right on his shoulders, denoting no special propensities'.

On the other side, for the Brownings, the Kinneys 'warmed our hearts' when they reported that Victor Emmanuel had expressed himself 'much gratified' by the references to his father, Charles Albert, in *Casa Guidi Windows*.

Mrs Kinney has an acute criticism in her *Memoir* of Browning as a poet: 'He labors in all he writes not to polish but to roughen.' She also has caustic remarks to make on members of the expatriate circle, how far inspired by jealousy of contacts with the Brownings it is difficult to know, as their presence casts a rose-coloured haze over the period and the people living in it. Of Robert Lytton, she wrote:

Young Bulwer affected Browningism, with its absurd efforts at originality but without Browning's latent power.... Both Brownings tolerated his intrusive man-worship with wonderful Christian (to be paradoxical) resignation: for at that time he was the most arrant coxcomb of a *littérateur*.

He and Isa, she says, were shadows that followed the Brownings around: she, 'who had been the intimate friend of Lord Bulwer-Lytton, senr., vivacious to the extreme and flippant of tongue, her admiration for the Brownings amounted to infatuation. ... They suffered her presence as they did that of Lytton.' Of Charles Lever she is more tolerant: forgiven no doubt, as so often, for his Irishness: he 'keeps always ahead of his means, and his chubby wife and daughters never think more than he does, beyond the frolic day'.

After later meetings the Brownings and the Kinneys grew to understand and like each other. On the question of spiritualism they divided off into William Kinney and Elizabeth as believers against Browning and Mrs Kinney as sceptics, but this only added to the enjoyment of frequent arguments in each other's rooms where they would be joined by Hiram Powers, a believer, but also a ready talker on any subject from medieval art to Swedenborgianism. Such conversation the Kinneys found 'a fountain of pure water in a land of infectious pools'.

The Americans were more shockable than the Brownings. When Robert announced with some satisfaction that George Sand had allowed him to kiss her hand when they met as she passed through Florence, Mrs Kinney asked disapprovingly:

'Pray, who is her lover now?'
'I can't say,' Browning replied, 'since she has a new one every day.'
'And *you* kiss the hand of such a woman – *Robert Browning* does this?'
'Yes, and *Elizabeth Barrett Browning* does the same in respect to one of the greatest geniuses God ever made.'

When Mrs Kinney went on to declare that the greater the genius, the greater the shame, Elizabeth protested 'as if my lips had spoken a blasphemy: "She is not a bad woman, but on the contrary a good and charitable one." '

The Brownings' ideas would no doubt have offended many of their friends if their fame had not forgiven them. Mrs Ogilvy also wrote about George Sand that she was amazed at Elizabeth's admiration for her and her pleasure that George Sand had kissed her in Paris. 'She [Elizabeth] was scandalized by my reply that such a kiss reminded me of Becky kissing Amelia when they met in later life. In truth, Mrs. Browning with all her genius had the simple purity of Thackeray's heroine.'

Elizabeth's tolerance for importunate visitors now resulted in an unfortunate friendship with Mr and Mrs Eckley, David and Sophia, rich Americans who sought out the Brownings, presenting them with expensive gifts and, to Browning's embarrassment, invitations to table-rappings in which Sophia declared herself a firm believer and claimed some mediumistic powers. She was yet another who had published slim volumes of verse and 'Meditations': also, a novel, *Orsilia*, was to come in 1867. These amateurish efforts never seemed to put Elizabeth off and in the case of Sophia she soon numbered her among friends she loved, not just liked: 'So delicate and refined with a peculiar and a most *delicate* affectionateness – more delicacy is impossible.' So devoted was she that later, in 1859, she wrote no less than eighty-six letters to her. Typical are beginnings such as: 'Dearest Sophie made of goodness'; 'First, I miss you, I miss you.'

At this time Elizabeth, so fascinated by spiritualism and anxious to believe, was ready to accept the testimony of witnesses who were not reliable nor of anything like her own intellectual calibre. She could have done with a gale of laughter from Landor to clear her mind; when Seymour Kirkup had tried to convert him he gave such a guffaw that the stone-deaf Kirkup heard it.

The summer they spent as usual above Bagni di Lucca where they enjoyed the informal life. Elizabeth wrote to Henrietta that it would shock Arabel if she came to stay: 'The irregularities of our house are scandalous – not immoral, observe, but scandalous.' It was worse when they visited London where she indulged Robert in his taste for company:

From morning till night people are running out and in – all sorts of people. There are men who come and talk – talk, some of them did last summer, till one in the morning and the freest sort of philosophy is talked. Fancy Mr. Stratten elbowed on the staircase by Mr. So-and-So whose 'aim in life' is to 'subvert Christianity'.

The Bohemian side of the girl who had scrambled down into the Boyds' garden, regardless of decorum, was even stronger now in Italy, for 'abroad' usually has a way of breaking down British inhibitions. She tells her sister how

Browning once opened the door to a countess before he had put on a neck tie, and she herself had received a grand duke with her hair down.

The visit to the Baths was overshadowed by the illness of the visiting Robert Lytton who had to be nursed by Browning and Isa Blagden. When Pen caught the infection, worry over this was another strain on Elizabeth's over-wrought nerves and she returned to Florence in October no better for the change. Another worry was to find a replacement for Wilson who was pregnant. In the event a girl called Annunciata was chosen and proved a great success as a younger, romping companion for Penini, happy to gabble in Italian with him and, no doubt, even happier to share his enthusiasm for any revolutionary soldiers they might meet on their walks.

During the autumn and winter of 1857–8 in Florence Elizabeth became very frail: she hardly left the apartment or only for short carriage drives. She was relieved to see Browning going out on his own in the evenings, for it was no hardship to her not to attend parties. In the long years before her marriage she had formed the habit of listening to other people's accounts of social life outside her sick room and enjoyed them. It was a form of her novel-reading. She did not feel in any sense neglected but rejoiced in the general appreciation of Browning's good looks and charm.

It was a blow when she heard that her father had died in April 1857 and left no message for her.*

She pulled herself out of depression, however, to receive Nathaniel Hawthorne whom she had met in London with Monckton Milnes. He had appealed to her for his interest in mesmerism and the occult, but by now he was rather bored with too much credulous talk about them. He described Elizabeth as 'of that quickly appreciative and responsive order of women', and said of Penini that he was as

---

* There is an elaborate memorial monument to him and his wife and daughter, Mary, in Ledbury parish church.

'un-English a production as if he were native of another planet'. And so he must have looked to such playmates as there were in the English and American colony, for he still had his long curls and wore 'Bubbles' clothes.

If this worried his father, he does not appear to have made any protest, but both parents were more concerned than they would have admitted at his lack of concentration. He was lively enough and enjoyed drawing and playing the piano but had no application. In this was he like Bro, who had given no sign of developing his talents? He spoke Italian as well as (or better than) English. Elizabeth encouraged this in her 'Florentine' as she liked to call him. Rather unexpectedly she did not start him on the Greek and Latin which she had so much enjoyed as a girl – in fact her interest in them seems to have lapsed, although Browning was something of a Greek scholar. This failure was to have unfortunate consequences later academically, as the Italian *abbé* brought in to teach him made little progress.

A bust of Pen was made at this time by Alexander Munro, an associate of the Pre-Raphaelite Brotherhood. He had contributed statues to Woodward's new science museum at Oxford and designed the tympanum for his Union building where Rossetti and his friends worked on the murals in 1857. When he went out to Rome and Florence it may have been Rossetti who introduced him to the Brownings, but anyway he soon met them and his admiration for Pen's looks ensured his acceptance. Both parents were delighted with the 'clay sketch' he made of the child. The bust in marble was shown at the Academy exhibition of 1859; 'he had the generosity', Elizabeth said, 'to insist on doing it for us at half price.' She begs Eliza Ogilvy to go and look at it in his studio when in London: 'it is beautiful and *tale quale*';* and to Munro she wrote: 'you must keep the bust for us for a time, because we want it to be seen before the Alps and Apennines shall cover it from the eyes of the north.' A note

* *Tale quale* may be colloquially translated as 'spit and image'.

from Browning years later to the sculptor when collecting the bust recalls nostalgically the Pen of those days, 'The Boy is a great fellow now out of curls and pretty collars and [I] shall be glad indeed of this bit of the old times.'

His parents were also pleased with the description of a child in Isa Blagden's novel, *Agnes Tremorne*, clearly based on him, where the features exactly resembled his mother's.

On Monday Giaconto resumed his sittings, and at ten o'clock he was duly stationed in the studio. He had washed his face, combed his long brown curls, and stuck a carnation in his round felt hat, which was his idea of making a *toilette*. . . .

He was a very pretty boy, not so much from regularity of features as general beauty of countenance. He had a broad, full, forehead, on each side of which his hair fell in long thick curls, and his eyes were large and bright and set wide apart. His mouth was well cut though somewhat large, and his teeth were white and even. . . . There was a peculiarity in his features such as one sometimes sees in the faces of children not destined to live till manhood: an entire compilation, as it were, of the infantine beauty.

But Pen was not to fulfil this feature of Victorian romantic convention.

# 16

# More Travels
# 1858

ELIZABETH once said that the only thing which did not tire
her was travel, so that she never hesitated to make these
moves about Italy and to Paris and London. A visit to Egypt
they did give up in the summer of 1858 as this really would
have been beyond her strength, but they set off in July again
for Paris via Leghorn and Marseilles. 'No more cypresses,'
Elizabeth wrote, 'no more fireflies, no more dreaming
repose on burning summer evenings. Push out the
churches, push in the boulevards.' Arabel Barrett came
over, so did George, and Alfred with his wife. It was sad in
other ways, for Lady Elgin whom they liked so much was
now paralysed and could not speak. In gratitude for her past
kindness, Browning gave up his time to go and read poetry
to her. Another friend in distress was Charles Sumner, the
American abolitionist, only slowly recovering from a
physical attack made upon him by a fellow Congressman in
Washington.

They so far obeyed doctor's orders as to linger no more
than two weeks in Paris but went on to Etretat and Le Havre
for the benefit of sea air. Elizabeth had nothing to do but 'to
sit on a bench and get strength, if it please God'. The nearest
to an adventure that the dull seaport provided was a visit to a

photographer's studio where she consented to be a victim in order that an engraving could be made from the result for a frontispiece to the fourth edition of *Aurora Leigh*. Browning was anxious that the Rossetti brothers should oversee the work and while he received progress reports from William Michael, copious instructions were sent to the engraver by Dante Gabriel. For him there was not only something wrong with the mouth (which needed 'a line of shadow all along the top of the upper lip'), the hair also was 'to be brought a little more down on the forehead with the parting line not left so raw'. Other features were to be altered too: even the line of the arm was to be 'considerably curved by adding to the sleeve' and he ended, more ominously than hopefully, that 'other modifications will be perceived'. All this makes it difficult to know whether the likeness is good or not.

A ten day visit from Joseph Milsand was very welcome to Browning, but apart from this both he and Elizabeth were bored with Le Havre and glad to leave for Paris on 20 September and go on from there back home to Florence.

How far Elizabeth could make light of any dangers in which they were involved when travelling shows in a letter she wrote when she found how worried friends in Florence had been at their delay in arriving. Indeed they had been involved in bad storms at sea from the Italian *burrasca*, a form of whirlwind.

Either we had perished by a railway accident on the Marseilles route (hinted at in a Galignani) or gone down in a steamer . . . or I had died on Mont Cenis and Robert had stopped to bury me at Turin. So that certain friends of ours were running about in a distracted way with pale faces – one confined to her room for four and twenty hours with fright.

When she went upstairs at Casa Guidi to their apartment, she met a friend coming down who stared aghast as if she had seen a ghost, 'an old inhabitant of the house haunting the ancient place'.

But once again they were to leave home, the doctors declaring that the climate of Rome would be better for Elizabeth in the winter and this was a prescription she was perfectly willing to accept.

In November 1858 they started travelling, this time more comfortably in a private carriage lent by the Eckleys, and found sunny and inexpensive rooms at 43 Bocca di Leone. Elizabeth was strong enough to attend Christmas Day High Mass at St Peter's in company with Browning and the inevitable Sophia. Their attendance at Roman Catholic services seems to have been undertaken as observers looking on at a ritual as alien as a primitive tribal dance. She described the experience in a New Year's letter to Ruskin:

> I was able to go out on Christmas morning (a wonderful event for me) and hear the silver trumpet in St. Peters. Well, it was fine. I never once thought of the Scarlet Lady nor of the Mortara* case nor anything to spoil the pleasure – yes and I enjoyed it, both aesthetically & devotionally, putting my own words to the music – was it wise, or wrong?

She did not realize that the depression in Ruskin's letter to her which she was answering was aggravated by a loss of Christian faith: Protestantism v. Catholicism meant little to him now. But towards Ruskin she was the respectful affectionate daughter that her own father had cast off, as she was a mother to the young Robert Lytton. With considerable sensitivity, she tried to cheer Ruskin by dwelling on the satisfaction that he ought to feel at all he had done. Had it been worth while, he asked, to have tried to help artists, all 'wrong-headed', or the ordinary breed of mankind 'always

---

* Edgar Mortara was a Jew whose nurse had him secretly baptized as a Roman Catholic in 1858. Protests from his family and from foreign governments could not persuade the Vatican to prosecute the nurse. After the capture of Rome in 1870 Mortara was given the opportunity to revert to Judaism but opted to become an Augustinian.

howling and bawling the right road to a generation of drunken cabmen'? Elizabeth replied with calm and confident assurance:

The sadness of your letter struck me like the languor after victory – for you who have fought many good fights never for a moment seemed to despond before, write this word and this. After treading the world down, in various senses, you are tired. It is natural perhaps but this evil will pass like other evils – and I wish from my heart a good clear noble year, with plenty of work, and God consciously over all to give you satisfaction.... I am what people call a 'mystic' and what I myself call a 'realist' because I consider that every step of the foot or stroke of the pen here has some real connection with a result in the hereafter.... and I dont think nothing is worth doing but that everything is worth doing.... everything good of course.... and that everything which does good after a moment does good for ever in *art* as well as in morals.

She refers with gratitude to his appreciation of her work: it is what really matters to her. When he wants anything in it changed she will do it for his sake.

Of course any remark of yours is to be received & considered with all reverence. Only, be sure you please to say: 'do it differently to satisfy *me*, John Ruskin,' and not to satisfy Mr. or Mrs. or the Miss and Master Smith of the great majority. The great majority is the majority of the little you know, who will come over to you if you dont think of them – and if they dont, you will bear it.

An élitist philosophy somewhat at variance with the doctrines of the Ruskin of *Unto This Last*, but of some personal comfort in this time of his mental overclouding.

Among Browning's social occasions was the official dinner given by the British ambassador for local celebrities to be presented to the Prince of Wales. He displayed suitably royal tact in recognizing the cultural interests of his expatriate subjects by saying he admired the portrait of Elizabeth by Field Talfourd which he had been to see, thus killing three birds with one stone.

Of this outside life of her husband's, Elizabeth wrote, 'So plenty of distractions, no "Men and Women" but men and women from without instead.' As a fellow artist she knew that people were necessary grist to his mill; for herself she more and more desired peace and rest. But what has been read into this as a death-wish should be taken in the context of the time, when world-weariness was as fashionable as *Werther*-melancholy had been earlier. And she made her own difficulties over being a recluse, for perversely she was always eager for news of the Italian revolt. 'Women don't generally break their hearts on these exterior subjects,' she wrote, 'but I am otherwise made.' In March 1860 her *Poems before Congress* was to be published; the title a misnomer, for the intended congress, to be held in Paris that January, never took place. She knew the book would be unpopular. As she wrote to Anna Jameson: 'Everybody will hate me for it, and so *you must* try to love me the more to make up for that.' And so it was indeed when the *Poems* appeared. *Blackwood's* referred to her 'poetic aberrations', and the *Saturday Review* called her 'a denationalised fanatic', an echo of *Blackwood's* earlier strictures on the second part of *Casa Guidi Windows*, when the reviewer said it showed the fair sex should remain angels and not become *tricoteuses*. There was additional hostility because 'A Curse for a Nation' was taken to refer to England, when she intended it for the slave states of America. Ironically it was from America now that she received an offer of one hundred dollars a time for any poem she chose to send to the New York *Independent*, which was generous as there was still no copyright agreement.

They returned to Florence in June. Here they found French troops in occupation as liberators and willingly contributed to the funds being raised for prosecution of *la guerra*. Elizabeth's enthusiasm for the French emperor seemed to be justified and this ensured better health and strength for her. But Browning dreaded a reaction.

To keep Penini from the overcharged atmosphere, he bought him a pony and engaged a manservant to look after it. The boy, for all the girlishness of his looks – and his clothes, for he still wore white embroidered drawers hanging below a tunic – was a fearless rider and managed his animal well. This must have gratified the John Bull/Englishman side of Browning who would also have backed his son's desire for a pair of coarse leather shoes to wear. Elizabeth does not seem to have been alarmed at such evidence of revolt against her prettifying of him and she still refused to consider sending him to school: he was not fit for it – 'he would be broken to pieces in it.'

Browning had another problem to sort out in the summer of 1859 when Landor, now eighty-four, was turned out of his villa at Fiesole by his family to whom, like King Lear, he had made over all his property. On a hot day in July, staggering down a dusty road with his wife's tirade of abuse echoing in his ears, he fortunately met Browning. He took charge of the old man and made Mrs Landor hand over some clothes and pieces of furniture and pictures. As Casa Guidi would not be a possible home, Browning was able to persuade him to go to the Storys at Sienna for a time. Proud as he was, Landor had less compunction in accepting their hospitality as they were obligated to him in several ways. But he wanted independence and Browning arranged for him to be installed in rooms kept by Wilson and her husband. The brothers in England provided an income which Browning had to control. Many of the old pre-Raphael pictures that Landor bought in markets or at fairs, despised at the time, are now rated highly.

The old lion was a trying lodger: he is said to have thrown his dinner out of the window and the servant after it, only expressing regret that he might have damaged the violets below. Elizabeth's initial dislike returned now that he no longer supported Louis Napoleon. The Storys found their encounters embarrassing:

Mrs. Browning, with her face hidden under her large hat and curls, would be stirred past endurance by these assaults upon her hero who was her 'Emperor for evermore' and would raise her treble voice even to a shrill pitch in protest until Mr. Browning would come into the fray as mediator.

For Landor who had written:

I strove with none, for none was worth my strife.
Nature I loved and, next to Nature, Art:
I warm'd both hands before the fire of life:
It sinks, and I am ready to depart.

the ashes grew cold. The evening of his life in Florence bore some resemblance to early days when he found an admiring friend to visit him daily in Isa Blagden and a pretty young woman, Kate Field, an American Rose Aylmer, to enjoy lessons in Latin. Eventually they had to move away and at the end he died lonely, cut off by loss of sight and hearing, aged eighty-nine in 1864. Boythorn into Lear without a Cordelia at the end.

# 17

# Last Years
# 1859–1861

AFTER he had settled Landor, Italian politics in July 1859 led to worse worry for Browning. A month following the rejoicing over French troops in Florence, the emperor suddenly concluded the Treaty of Villafranca by which he surrendered to Austria most of what they had won. This dealt a blow to Elizabeth almost literally mortal, for it brought on 'violent palpitations and a cough' such as she had not known since coming to Italy. Browning stayed up with her every night and took over Pen's lessons in the mornings.

A change of scene was, as ever, the doctors' recommendation and Siena was decided upon. They were able to rent the Villa Alberti again, with its views over 'deep purple hills with intermediate tracts of green vineyards'. Browning had to carry Elizabeth in his arms from the carriage, but she soon rallied and began to go out every day for a drive while Pen rode his pony boldly for two or three hours. Sociable by nature, he also enjoyed sitting in ox carts, on top of the manure, chatting to the peasants.

The Storys were nearby with Landor in a separate cottage but otherwise the Brownings were happy to be free of visitors 'dropping in'. An exception was made for the diplomat, Odo Russell (nephew of Lord John), who had been 'heartbroken' at not finding them in Florence. They felt they must offer to accommodate him for a night. Elizabeth admitted she flew at him for the British government's policy of non-intervention in the Italian revolt. She had admired Russell in the days of his Reform Bill but now attacked his attitude as 'old fogeyism'. Odo Russell defended it on the grounds that England had no power to interfere. 'He admits it with a smooth accent and countenance,' she wrote to Henrietta, apologizing for dwelling on politics, 'while I revolt against the fact and call it intolerably hideous, a national sin crying out for judgement.'

In October they were back in Florence but left for Rome in November where they were met at the outskirts by the Storys, now living in a wing of the Palazzo Barberini, naïvely described by the young Anny Thackeray as 'grander than Windsor Castle, with sun rippling all down the marble steps'. In the studio there Story was working on two statues, 'Cleopatra' and the 'Libyan Sibyl', that were to have a great success at the 1862 Exhibition in London. (These and his 'Medea' are now in Goldsmiths' Hall, London, and his statue of George Peabody is by the Royal Exchange.) Browning was glad of his companionship and willing to enjoy again the eccentricities of Madame Mohl who used to 'drop in on them out of an omnibus, often into a mud-puddle at our door and delight us with her originality and ideas'. She would stay to talk for hours, with feet on the fender, in a 'state of general untidiness', as Story called it, 'so marked as to be picturesque'.

From Browning's going about more the Italians recognized him and Elizabeth as friends who supported the cause of liberation and they were invited as 'poets and lovers of Italy' to visit Castellani's famous jeweller's shop to admire the sword made secretly for presentation by grateful Romans to Victor Emmanuel of Piedmont, now king of a united Italy. This honour encouraged them to involve themselves actively so far as to allow patriots to come to their apartment to read forbidden newspapers.

Back home in Florence in June 1860 they received the unhappy news of Anna Jameson's death earlier in the year. She was the best friend that Elizabeth ever had. Independent in mind and a hard, if uninspired, worker at her books, she never craved an intimacy that could become demanding. And there was never to be forgotten the sympathy and practical help that she had shown to Elizabeth and Robert on what might be called their elopement.

Very different was another woman who was now to deal Elizabeth a blow deeply wounding. Sophia Eckley confessed that she had never had any mediumistic powers and had invented the experiences she reported. As an impostor she probably had no inkling of what this revelation would mean to someone who was a would-be believer struggling to suppress doubts. From certain feelings of guilt at her own obstinacy in refusing to look facts in the face, particularly her husband's warnings, and to ask relevant questions, Elizabeth was pitiless to the friend who had betrayed her. The sweetness she had liked became cloying: 'floods of tears, floods' annoyed and did not move her. She extended her impatience to other women who approached her: 'They come to me, lay themselves under my feet – and end by tripping me up.' She also wrote a short poem called 'Where's Agnes?' based on her disillusionment:

> She, who scarcely trod the earth,
> Turned mere dirt? My Agnes, – mine!

But, miserable as 1860 was for Elizabeth, weak in health and depressed from these blows, the month of July is notable for her future reputation as it saw the publication in the *Cornhill*, under Thackeray's editorship, of her best-loved poem, 'A Musical Instrument' (not to be confused with the much-earlier 'The Dead Pan'). In this she fulfils herself.

What was he doing, the great god Pan,
  Down in the reeds by the river?
Spreading ruin and scattering ban,
Splashing and paddling with hoofs of a goat,
And breaking the golden lilies afloat
  With the dragon-fly on the river.

He hacks at the reeds till he finds the one he wants and then trims it.

He cut it short, did the great god Pan,
  (How tall it stood in the river!),
Then drew the pith, like the heart of a man,
Steadily from the outside ring,
And notched the poor dry empty thing
  In holes, as he sate by the river.

'This is the way,' laughed the great god Pan
  (Laughed while he sate by the river),
'The only way, since gods began
To make sweet music, they could succeed.'
Then, dropping his mouth to the hole in the reed,
  He blew in power by the river.

In the last verse of the poem a note of human doubt creeps in: joy cannot be wholly without loss and pain.

Yet half a beast is the great god Pan,
To laugh as he sits by the river,
Making a poet out of a man:
The true gods sigh for the cost and pain, –
For the reed which grows nevermore again
  As a reed with the reeds in the river.

The philosophy of this was questioned by Anthony Trollope, writing to his brother: the making of a poet should not mar the man. 'A man that can be a poet is so much more a man in becoming such and is the more fitter for a man's best work.' All the old love of philosophical argument in which Elizabeth had engaged as a girl with Mr Boyd re-emerged in her reply addressed to Thomas Trollope: the poet, she insists, does destroy the instrument, that is, himself, in the reed he uses. 'The poetic organisation', she wrote, 'implies certain disadvantages: for instance an exaggerated susceptibility,' and the loss of privacy, 'of sweet unconscious cool privacy among the reeds, which I for one can so long for'. But Trollope was right. In this poem, so nearly her last, she fulfilled herself. Early weaknesses and affectations are put aside; there is no seeking after made-up compounds, no discordant rhymes and no more costume subjects, romaunts and the like, but a statement put to music in simple notes. She shows her understanding of the artist's dilemma and, although she does not make the claim, the poem proves she overcame it as woman and as poet. In the haunting lines, the meaning is in their magic.

One event on a day in June that was to have a momentous consequence was the purchase by Browning of a certain 'square old yellow book' from a stall of odds-and-ends in the square. He 'gave a lira for it, eightpence English just'. Eight years later the story it told was to become his masterpiece, *The Ring and the Book*.

They went to Rome again in November, to 126 Via Felice, where news came in December of the death of Henrietta. It was a merciful release after a prolonged and painful illness, during which Elizabeth bitterly regretted she had not been in a fit state herself to travel to England to see her sister and be of some help to the husband and children. She did not indulge her grief, however, but received certain Englishmen travelling to Rome: John Bowring among them, a statesman who began as a liberal internationalist but ended by involving his country in what was regarded as an unacceptable piece of imperial bullying when he decided against the Cantonese in the *Arrow* affair. There was to be a parallel nearly a hundred years later at the time of Suez.

The British consul in Rome at this time was Joseph Severn and Elizabeth was eager to meet him, to hear all details possible about Keats who had died in his arms forty years before at the little house on the corner of Piazza di Spagna. 'I made him tell me the most minute details – some very painful.'

Entirely happy was the visit of Hans Andersen, as beloved by children in life as in literature. He used to carry about with him pieces of broken toy soldiers given to him by children when they could spare the precious fragments. At the Storys' there took place a famous children's party when he read the *Ugly Duckling* and *Story with a Flute*, playing the Pied Piper as he led the children all round the rooms of the Palazzo Barberini. The last verses that Elizabeth wrote, 'The North and the South', were in honour of Andersen. A dialogue between North and South, it ends:

> The North sent therefore a man of men
>     As a grace to the South;
> And thus to Rome came Andersen.
> – *'Alas, but must you take him again?'*
>     Said the South to the North.

In 1861 they followed the same routine of leaving Rome for Florence before the hot weather. Here they were met by the news of the death of Cavour on 6 June – a blow which Elizabeth felt as keenly as a personal loss, and which worsened her weakened state of health. In regard to Cavour, she and Browning were agreed. He had lacked the romantic aura, the charisma, of Mazzini and Garibaldi in their different ways, but he had been the wisest of the leaders: at once shrewd and honest. It was reasonable, if not popular, to trade Savoy and Nice to Napoleon in exchange for Tuscany and Modena, and he had been farsighted enough to see the troubles that would arise from incorporating Sicily and the south in a united Italy.

Correspondence was so much a part of Elizabeth's life that two letters may be symbolically quoted here for her last months. One that she received from Mrs Harriet Beecher Stowe pleased her, as it told how she had been able to communicate at a seance with her dead son. Support from such a source was an encouragement to Elizabeth's faith for she much admired Mrs Stowe. She had at once recognized her world bestseller, *Uncle Tom's Cabin*, as 'the most successful book printed by man or woman'.

One letter of Elizabeth's that lay unfinished on her desk was to Jessie White Mario, the Englishwoman married to an exiled Italian who went to nurse Garibaldi's Redshirts when the Thousand marched on Rome. From her she must have heard too of John Whitehead Peard from Cornwall, known as 'Garibaldi's Englishman', who helped to organize his irregular bands and at times impersonated him in the villages to rouse the peasants to join them.

When, back at Casa Guidi, Elizabeth was too weak to get up, Browning carried her out for a short time on to the balcony to see across to San Felice which he and she had loved looking at through all the years they had lived there. Isa Blagden was one of the few friends allowed to see her and in the afternoon of 28 June called to bring the latest Italian news to which Elizabeth listened with all her old interest. Browning was out so Isa took it on herself to shut a window which she thought was causing a draught in spite of the warmth of the season. Afraid to tire her friend she left after a short visit.

Frail as she seemed, Elizabeth insisted that she was no worse than on other occasions when doctors had said her lungs were affected. 'I am always dying and it makes no difference,' she had written to Henrietta five years before. She talked about leaving Casa Guidi, now too cramped with Pen growing up, and joining the Storys at another flat in the Barberini. She was also eager to discuss plans for the usual summer move, whether to Siena again or to try Switzerland. Clearly she had no premonition of what was to come, though Browning, less sanguine, insisted on sitting up with her at night.

On the evening of Friday, the twenty-eighth, Lytton

called but stayed to talk only with Browning. Isa Blagden, however, was admitted to Elizabeth's room. She had come with some new item of political news. Browning forbade such talk for fear of the harm excitement could cause, but Elizabeth contrived to whisper behind his back. Isa thought she was better, as did Wilson who called, and the doctor also.

That evening when Pen came to her bedside to bid her his usual two goodnights he asked if she were really better.

'Much better,' she told him.

But during the early hours she awoke and Browning immediately went over to her. She assured him that it was nothing and they talked for a time of the life they had shared together. When she became drowsy he held her in his arms.

'Are you comfortable?' he asked her.

'Beautiful,' she replied, but her head drooped and she fell silent.

She had had fits of fainting before but this time he knew it was the end. She died without pain in the early hours of 29 June 1861.

Story recorded Browning's words as he looked round the rooms he was never to visit again:

'The cycle is complete, here we came fifteen years ago; here Pen was born; here Ba wrote her poems for Italy. She used to walk up and down this verandah in the summer evenings, when, revived by the southern air, she first again began to enjoy her out-doors life. Every day she used to walk with me or drive with me, and once even walked to Bellosguardo and back; that was when she was strongest. Little by little, as I now see, that distance was lessened, the active out-doors life restricted, until walking had finally ceased. We saw from these windows the return of the Austrians; they wheeled round this corner and came down this street with all their cannon, just as she describes it in "Casa Guidi". Last week when we came to Florence I said: "We used, you know, to walk on this verandah so often – come and walk up and down once. Just once," I urged, and she came to the window and took two steps on it but it fatigued her too much, and she went back and lay down on the sofa – that was our last walk.'

Elizabeth's death deprived Robert Browning of his mission. His purpose in life gone, he was never wholly at peace with himself again. He was still a poet – *The Ring and the Book* established him as a major one – but that he sought distraction in social contacts and correspondence with women admirers showed his essential loneliness. The slim dandy of his young manhood became the stout diner-out, uncertain of his identity.

In *The Ring and the Book*, which appeared eight years after Browning had found that little yellow volume on the market stall, he went back to the years of fulfilment and dedicated it to his dead wife in remembrance of the love that had endured between them.

> O lyric Love, half angel and half bird
> And all a wonder and a wild desire, ...
> Hail then, and hearken from the realms of help!
> Never may I commence my song, my due
> To God who best taught song by gift of thee,
> Except with bent head and beseeching hand –
> That still, despite the distance and the dark,
> What was, again may be; some interchange
> Of grace, some splendour once thy very thought,
> Some benediction anciently thy smile!

Browning's relationship with Penini was uneasy until Pen's marriage to the American Fannie Coddington brought reconciliation and a settled home where Robert was always welcome. Fannie adored her father-in-law (had she married Pen because he was his son?) and the memory of E.B.B. She was able to place a copy of *Asolando* in his hands on his deathbed for it was with her and Pen at the magnificent Palazzo Rezzonico in Venice that Browning died in 1889.

From a younger generation of English couples in Italy comes a description of Browning's funeral.

We [the Hultons] went to the funeral service at the Palace. His coffin stood in the centre of the great hall, covered with a purple pall with a simple wreath of laurel resting on it. Then we followed in the gondola procession to San Michele where his remains were deposited pending their removal to England. As we passed under the Rialto bridge the setting sun burst out of the clouds which had covered the sky all that day and shone with fantastic lights upon the funeral barge and the gilded ornaments.*

\* From unpublished memoir of Costanza Hulton, step-daughter of Senator Pasquale Villari, mother of Teresa (Lady Berwick) who was god-daughter of Fannie Browning.

# APPENDIX I

# What Happened Afterwards to Penini

WITH a parentage so out of the ordinary and an unusual upbringing, Penini's future is bound to arouse curiosity. In an atmosphere of sententiousness and apportionment of blame, perhaps the flippant couplet which sums it all up may be excused:

> Sons of great men all remind us
> We should leave no heirs behind us.

So much of the Brownings' life followed in the footsteps of the Shelleys that it is not irrelevant here to compare Penini with their son, Percy Florence, who became as ordinary as his mother could wish. In her widowhood, when Mary Shelley was reproached for sending him to a conventional school like Harrow, she declared that she wanted nothing better for him than to be 'like other people', for she had suffered enough from a father and a husband who were mavericks, at odds with the world. Percy Florence had artistic talent; he was a tolerable water-colourist and designed scenery for his stage at Boscombe Manor. His friends were literary, the most notable among them Robert Louis Stevenson whom he entertained on his yacht (a far cry from his father's fated *Don Juan*) and other writers and artists of minor importance in their day. He made a happy marriage which lasted until the end of his life.

Similarly Pen had talent not genius. He was quite good as a sculptor (a pupil of Rodin's at one time), and his painting was praised by Millais and Alma Tadema among others. But with him there was always the lingering doubt: did they praise his work to please his father? He did not paint scenery for any theatre but was a remarkable 'interior decorator', as it would now be called. He restored the Tiepolo ceiling at the Palazzo Rezzonico and himself painted vast murals there. Under-sized in physique, he compensated by huge artistic enterprises but he also executed charming easel paintings.

A really beautiful child, he grew into a plain man and the confidence behind the easy manners that had won him admiration in Italy, was sapped later when he felt that people meeting him for the first time were disappointed, saying to themselves and not always disguising their feelings, 'Is this the son of those two?'

Always amiable, he kept on affectionate terms with his Aunt Arabel, who mothered him when his father brought him back to England. But he felt as alien there as the Aurora of his mother's poem when she stood on the deck of the ship taking her away from Italy:

> ... In all a child's astonishment at grief
> Stared at the wharf-edge where she stood and moaned,
> My poor Assunta, where she stood and moaned!
> The white walls, the blue hills, my Italy. ...

Assunta here could stand for his own Annunciata and all the peasants he had met on his holidays or the urchins in Florence that he invited back to his home.

Faithful to old friends, he kept in touch with Wilson and Ferdinando and indeed employed them at the Palazzo, and had his aunt, Sarianna, to live with him till her death, but in early manhood he made no lasting friendships and his marriage to Fannie Coddington broke up. In spite of joining house parties with Millais in Scotland and being on easy terms with acquaintances in the sporting world, he was always more at home with his social inferiors.

His career at Oxford, where Browning got him accepted at Christ Church, as his classics were not up to the standard that Benjamin Jowett expected at Balliol, was a disaster. Or was it simply a case of high expectations not fulfilled? After all, plenty of undergraduates were 'ploughed' and sent down. It was not the end of the world. But to Browning it was. Added to the academic failure was the fact that he had got into an undesirable set. As a good oarsman and a champion at billiards he did not make the sort of friends that his father could approve. He also ran badly into debt.

It is not known for certain why his marriage to Fannie broke up. She adored her father-in-law and the memory of Elizabeth so that she must subconsciously have wished that Penini resembled them more. When she left him it may have been because of his extravagance, or, on his side, he may have lost patience with her fits of hysteria or, most likely, she refused to tolerate his infidelities. There are letters extant between ladies of the English and American colony in Venice which show they regarded her as a woman wronged. One Italian woman, with a Gallic attitude to such things, declared any wife was a fool not to expect her husband to be unfaithful. One thing in regard to Pen is quite certain and that is that, against all Freudian doctrine, his mother's treatment of him did not make him homosexual. On the contrary, though nothing can be confirmed, there were rumours throughout his life of affairs with women, beginning with the seduction of a Breton peasant girl when he was nineteen and suspicion of several illegitimate children later on.

Pen has been said to have been 'spoilt'. He was certainly uncommonly indulged but if he had been harshly treated he would be equally regarded as 'spoilt', and so made into a delinquent. Whatever parents do is wrong.

The end of Pen's life considered on its own, without regard to inherited or environmental influences, was a placidly useful one. He settled at Asolo and organized there a home lace-making industry. He was much loved by the people and for his services to the district was made *Cavaliere della Corona d'Italia*. He died on 8 June 1912.

# APPENDIX II

# *Aurora Leigh*: Narrative and Themes

*Aurora Leigh* must be considered on its own, for it is on this epic novel in verse that Elizabeth Barrett Browning wished her reputation to rest. It is her *magnum opus* and, if not autobiographical, it contains her theories about life and art with particular reference to the life of the woman artist. It might enjoy a wider public nowadays if it had been written in prose for there would then have been less indulgence in some of the *longueurs* which are no longer acceptable. Most Victorian novels have either lengthy or fanciful descriptions of natural surroundings, which few readers will not have been guilty of skipping, but here it is the passages of aesthetic moralizing that fail to hold the attention. The scenery is of interest because it is based so exactly on the countryside in which Elizabeth grew up and shows how deeply she cherished the memory of her girlhood home, although she never went back there. She draws comparisons between the Italy she came to love and the gently rising mounds of Hope End with the Malvern Hills beyond them:

> (As if God's finger touched but did not press
> In making England), such an up and down
> Of verdure, – nothing too much up or down,
> A ripple of land; such little hills, the sky
> Can stoop to tenderly and the wheat fields climb.

Her lack of sympathy with her native country is forgone when she recalls the years she spent in Herefordshire, disguised as Shropshire in describing the Leigh estate.

As a novel *Aurora Leigh* has a theme, the characters develop and clues are laid to hold the interest and point to what is coming. In the first two books the main characters, Aurora and her cousin, Romney Leigh, are shown in their arrogant youth. Aurora, a half-Italian orphan adopted by an English aunt, is full of spiritual pride, convinced that the world can be saved by art and that she is to be the saviour. Her cousin, Romney, in love with her, is more attractive but equally obstinate in his conviction that he must also save the world, not by art which he tends to despise, but by social service:

> ... fevered with dreams of doing good
> To good-for-nothing people.

He asks her to marry him as a helpmate but she refuses.

> Sir, you were married long ago.
> You have a wife already whom you love,
> Your social theory.

There is feminine pique here as well as ideological disagreement. The aunt is very angry as she sees in the marriage a safeguard for her ward's future. The aunt is well drawn with an acerbity that creeps into Elizabeth's verse more often than is generally appreciated. She can hardly have been modelled on Aunt Bummy, who seems to have been a bit of a bumbler, but perhaps more on Aunt Jane (Hedley) who had taken a narrow view of the Browning marriage, perhaps a little too on sister Arabel, but probably most on the sort of women on whom she had had to make those boring calls as a girl,

> The poor club exercised her Christian gifts
> Of knitting stockings, stitching petticoats,
> Because we are of one flesh after all

And need one flannel (with a proper sense
Of difference in the quality).

There are other lines that emphasize this note of rebellion against middle-class convention. Aurora's reception, by the aunt, for instance, when as a child she arrives from Florence after her father's death (her mother had been an Italian actress much disapproved of by the English Leigh relations).

                                                    I, alas,
A wild bird scarcely fledged, was brought to her cage,
    And she was there to meet me. Very kind.
Bring the fresh water, give out the fresh seed.

Aurora withdrew into herself:

        I was a good child on the whole,
            A meek and manageable child. . . .

The aunt was not a cruel stepmother but kind according to her lights:

                    . . . she owned
    She liked a woman to be womanly,
    And English women, she thanked God and sighed
    (Some people always sigh in thanking God),
    Were models to the universe.

Another picture by Arthur Hughes, commissioned by Ellen Heaton, shows Aurora rejecting Romney, with the figure of the aunt in the distance. Formerly called 'The Tryst' it is now more appropriately entitled 'The Parting'.

In Book III the aunt is dead, unable to leave any income to Aurora as without a male heir the Leigh estate went to Romney. Aurora, determined on independence, goes to London where she endures a certain amount of hardship but before too long makes a name for herself and begins to move in the sort of circles where she hears of Romney's reputation and meets some of his friends. Sarcastically his activities are described:

His phalansteries there, his speeches here,
    His pamphlets, pleas, and statements everywhere.…

Aurora does not get much enjoyment from her fame or her fans. She opens her letters:

Blanche Ord, the writer in the 'Lady's Fan'
Requests my judgment on … that, afterwards.
Kate Ward desires the model for my cloak.…

There are the beggars and the young aspirants: girls and youths. One comes:

With pretty maiden seals, – initials twined
Of lilies, or a heart marked *Emily*
(Convicting Emily of being all heart);
Or rarer tokens from young bachelors,
Who wrote from college with the same goosequill,
Suppose, they had just been plucked of, and a snatch
From Horace, 'Collegisse juvat', set
Upon the first page.

With her position established she sometimes consents to attend aristocratic receptions, making out that she sits patiently in a corner looking on at the society beauties and overhearing the gossip. In one piece of satire she listens to a young German student, 'hair parted in the middle', holding forth to a patient older man of no great intellectual pretensions, Sir Blaise. The student is overcome by the beauty of Lady Waldemar:

… 'Beautiful!'
My student murmured rapt, – 'Mark how she stirs!
Just waves her head, as if a flower indeed,
Touched far off by the vain breath of our talk.'

There is another well-known character in Lady Howe, wife of the only aristocrat Aurora is prepared to tolerate and to forgive for his worldly cynicism. She is a woman who has subordinated her own interests in order to be the perfect hostess, as Aurora might have become the perfect partner for Romney and been equally bored to death, the female lifeblood in her frozen.

> His wife is gracious, with her glossy braids,
> And even voice, and gorgeous eyeballs, calm
> As her other jewels. If she's somewhat cold
> Who wonders, when her blood has stood so long
> In the ducal reservoir she calls her line
> By no means arrogantly? she's not proud;
> Not prouder than the swan is of the lake
> He has always swum in: – 'tis her element:
> And so she takes it with a natural grace
> Ignoring tadpoles....

At the same time Romney has carried his social conscience to the extreme of offering to marry a girl he has rescued from a sweatshop, Marian Erle. Trying to save him from himself, the beautiful Lady Waldemar appeals to Aurora for help but receives a dusty answer. All the same, Aurora goes to visit the girl and her slum dwelling is graphically described, perhaps from what Elizabeth knew of the visit to rescue Flush or just that the dirt and noise of one deprived neighbourhood does not vary much from another in literary time or place. She talks to the girl, who has had a thoroughly unhappy life, and seems to feel that Romney would be better off with her than with the frivolous Lady Waldemar.

There is then a scene in Book IV that would be first-rate in any novel and that is in the church where the wedding is to take place. It is said to be in Pimlico but sounds like St George's, Hanover Square (no less). Romney in his naïvety is determined to invite both his society friends and Marian's neighbours. As it is emphasized how much she has a soul above her surroundings, they must have been more protégés of Romney's than intimates of hers. Anyway,

Romney's idea is to provide them with a rich marriage feast on Hampstead Heath after the ceremony.

Aurora attends. As an onlooker she notes that the society women behave in their fashion worse than any of the slum-dwellers, standing up on the pews to look at them across the nave while holding perfumed handkerchiefs to their delicate nostrils.

The tittle-tattle while the congregation waits, again would suit a satirical novel. Conjectures and questions about Marian fly round.

> 'They say the bride's a mere child, who can't read
> But knows the things she shouldn't, with wide-awake
> Great eyes.'

There is gossip about fashionable love affairs, and a swipe at neglectful MP's:

> 'Adair, you stayed for the Division?' 'Lost
> By one.' 'The devil it is! I'm sorry for't'....
> 'Constituents must remember, after all,
> We're mortal.'

The delay grows intolerable. Each side fidgets: the rich anxious to get away to their luncheon parties, the poor hungry for Hampstead Heath.

> 'Ah, there she comes,
> The bride at last!' 'Indeed, no. Past eleven.
> She puts off her patched petticoat to-day
> And puts on Mayfair manners, so begins
> By setting us to wait.'

Marian never turns up. There is a riot when the slum guests think they will therefore be done out of the feast and attack Romney as if it were all his fault. Aurora rushes to try to save him (one of the clues that point to her latent love for him) until pulled back by Lord Howe who rescues both her and Romney.

The last sight left to me
Was Romney's terrible calm face above
The tumult!

In the fifth and following books, up until the final ninth,
'the plot thickens' with Lady Waldemar pursuing Romney
unscrupulously. She persuades Marian that she ought to
give up Romney and the girl consents. With seeming kindness Lady Waldemar promises money for the fare to
Australia in the care of an ex-maid of her own. Marian is
suspicious of this woman when she calls on her, but trusting
to the superior knowledge, as she thinks it, of an educated
lady of title, she consents to go and finds herself trapped and
confined in a brothel in Paris. The field is now clear except
for Aurora, whom Lady Waldemar senses as a rival with
more insight than Aurora herself shows.

Lady Waldemar is genuinely in love with Romney. For
his sake she has refused to marry men richer and of higher
social standing, and has made gallant efforts to keep up with
his interests. Subscribing to his various charities was easier
for her than reading his propaganda. She tells Aurora:

I read half Fourier through,
Proudhon, Considérant, and Louis Blanc,
With various others of his Socialists,
And, if I had been a fathom less in love,
Had cured myself with gaping. . . .

Aurora, tired of London fame, decides to visit Italy and
on the way stops in Paris (as the Brownings so often did).
There by chance she is able to track down Marian by catching a glimpse of her in a flower market and following her
home. The girl now has a baby son. Aurora shows a certain
obtuseness in her shock at seeing the child and the mother's
devotion to him.

'You found him, Marian?'
'Aye, I found him where
I found my curse – in the gutter with my shame.'

Aurora is reluctant to condone this, so reflecting an attitude of the time which considered seduction must have involved some pleasure or at least some profit. Marian is furious: she did not fall to temptation nor enjoy the seduction. On the contrary it was by brute force at the brothel that she had become pregnant.

> 'What, "seduced"'s your word?
> Do wolves seduce a wandering fawn in France?
> Do eagles, who have pinched a lamb with claws,
> Seduce it into carrion? So with me.
> I was not ever, as you say, seduced,
> But simply, murdered.'

Aurora, convinced, takes Marian and the child with her to Florence where she relaxes in the congenial surroundings and enjoys at a distance news of the great success her *magnum opus* (we are not told what) is having in London. She is content to rest on the laurels she has won there and now to be an onlooker at life, watching the Florentine Pippas pass.

She takes leisurely walks, about –

> ... the narrow, unrecognising streets,
> Where many a palace-front peers gloomily
> Through stony vizors iron-barred (prepared
> Alike, should foe or lover pass that way,
> For guest or victim)....

or visits the churches, seeing with a novelist's eye the worshippers there. A little hunchback:

> The pitiful black kerchief round her neck
> Sole proof she had had a mother,

a young woman sick for love because she has lost Gigi to Giuliana, and a poor old woman still hoping that some luck will come her way:

> 'And yet, now even, if Madonna willed,
> She'd win a tern in Thursday's lottery....'

Naturally the novel cannot stop there. Inevitably one evening she is sitting on her terrace when she is startled to hear the voice of Romney Leigh near at hand. She had taken it for granted he had married Lady Waldemar.

'You, Romney! – Lady Waldemar is here?'

He puts off his reply and the talk he is determined to have with her till she invites him to sit down.

> 'Will you sit?' I asked,
> And motioned to a chair; but down he sate,
> A little slowly, as a man in doubt,
> Upon the couch beside me. . . .

This is the first of the clues leading up to the dénouement: others follow when she refers to the bright hopes of their youth and the disappointments and disillusion each has suffered since.

> 'I'm thinking, Romney, how 'twas morning then,
> And now 'tis night.'

To which there comes an echo:

> 'And now,' he said ''tis night.'

And later when she talks of the starry sky:

> 'Aye,' he said, ''tis night. . . .
> You have the stars,' he murmured, 'it is well:
> Be like them! shine, Aurora, on my dark. . . .'

Aurora still thinks he is married to Lady Waldemar, for a letter from Lord Howe with news that there had been no marriage had never reached her. But Romney does consider himself bound in marriage still to Marian Erle. On over-hearing this the girl comes forward and says she does not wish ever to marry; she may respect but she does not love Romney and she wants no more children to compete with her boy.

> She was gone.

Romney feels Aurora still does not love him and prepares to leave. He does not regret his love for her all these years – he swears it:

> 'I attest
> Those stars above us which I cannot see.'

At last Aurora realizes he is blind, but tries to push the fact away from her:

> 'Speak once, Romney. 'Tis not true.
> I hold your hands, I look into your face –
> You see me?' 'No more than the blessed stars,
> Be blessed too, Aurora.'

His blindness changes everything. She had loved him all along and now is ready to devote her life to him and, as it were, pool their ideals, her art and his good works, for the benefit of the world.

> Beloved, let us love so well
> Our work shall be the better for our love.

It cannot be ignored here that Elizabeth was accused of plagiarism by having Romney blinded like Charlotte Brontë's Rochester and under somewhat similar circumstances. She herself repudiated the suggestion and had so little recollection of *Jane Eyre* that she had to send out for a copy to look it up. Post-Freud may come the idea that blinding the hero is a form of female revenge, mutilation of the superior being, but it is more likely that Charlotte Brontë and E. B. B. used the device as a way of rounding off their stories. In a later bestseller, *The Rosary* by Florence Barclay, the hero is conveniently blinded so that he can be nursed (possessed?) by the heroine who was too plain to attract him when he had his sight.

# APPENDIX III

# 'A Night-watch by the Sea'*

The ocean wheels around in circles of low sound,
    Around the rocky basement:
And every midnight long, distinct as human song,
    I hear it by the casement.
Oh, many many be anear unto the sea,
    The waker and the dreamer –
While ever ever low, the water measures go
    Beneath the moony glimmer.
There watcheth in the house the fisher's widow'd spouse –
    There prayeth soft the muser –
The nurse that came for hire, nods besides the sick man's fire,
    Whose eyes grow dark and lose her:
A poet sleepeth calm, with meek brow on his arm,
    Though shadow'd by the wreathing –
Two children, mouth to mouth! – sweetest mouths! the redder
both
    For warmth of mutual breathing!
But the corpse lies all alone, and never, more than stone,
    Sigh or motion can be giving –
And to-morrow, all alone, they will leave it 'neath the stone,
    When the priest hath bless'd the living.

* From the *Monthly Chronicle*, April 1840. Reproduced here as not readily
accessible.

The fisher's widow'd spouse, she watcheth in the house
    To weep – no more to hearken!
Loving angels seem to say sweet amens to those who pray,
    In tones the wave is working –
Nods the nurse to every tone, little thinking how upon
    Her charge, the death is winning, –
While the sick man, dreamingly, takes the rushing of the sea
    For eternity beginning!
And that rushing is bewild'ring the poet and the children
    With dream-voices in love measure,
Till the little children stir, like the birds in sunny air,
    Made uneasy with a pleasure!
But the corpse lies deaf and still, with its feet toward the hill,
    And its ear to the sea-murmur, –
Nor, though stormy winds should bring a louder murmuring
    Than the present or the former,
Sound or vision will it have, – till the trump outsounds the wave
    Where the wormwood star descended:
And with one foot on the sea, and a lifted hand to *Thee*,
Thine angel, by the secret of Thine own eternity,
    Shall swear that Time is ended!

# A Chronology of the Brownings' Travels

*(Courtesy of Philip Kelley, from 'The Brownings' Correspondence, A Checklist', 1978)*

1846

| | |
|---|---|
| 19 Sept | London – Le Havre |
| 20 Sept | Le Havre – Rouen |
| 21 Sept | Rouen – Paris (1 night at Hotel Messageries, then to Hotel de la Ville de Paris) |
| 28 Sept | Left Paris for |
| 29 Sept | Orléans; then via Bourges & Roanne to Lyons |
| 6 Oct | Left Lyons for Avignon |
| 8 Oct | Vaucluse, then via Aix-en-Provence to Marseilles |
| 11 Oct | Embarked for Genoa |
| 12 Oct | Arrived Genoa |
| 13 Oct | Left Genoa for Leghorn |
| 14 Oct | Leghorn – Pisa (three days at Hotel Peverada) |
| 18 Oct | Collegio di Ferdinando, Pisa |
| 31 Dec | |

1847

| | |
|---|---|
| 1 Jan | Collegio di Ferdinando, Pisa |
| 19 Apr | |
| 20 Apr | To Florence (2 days at Hotel du Nord) |
| 22 Apr | Moved to 4222 Via delle Belle Donne |
| 14 July | To Vallombrosa (5 days) |
| 19 July | Returned to Florence (4222 Via delle Belle Donne) |
| 20 July | Moved to Casa Guidi |
| 19 Oct | To 1881 Via Maggio (10 days) then to Piazza Pitti |

1848

| | |
|---|---|
| 9 May | Moved back to Casa Guidi |
| 17 July | Florence to Arezzo, Fano (3 days), Ancona (1 week), Loreto (1 day), Sinigallia, Fano, Pesaro, Rimini, Ravenna, Forli, and back to Florence (Casa Guidi). Away three weeks |

1849

| | |
|---|---|
| June | Florence – Pisa – Carrera – Spezia (2 days) – Seravezza – Bagni di Lucca (1 day). Away 5 days |
| 30 June | To Bagni di Lucca (Casa Valeri, Bagni Caldi) |
| 17 Oct | Arrived back at Casa Guidi |

1850

| | |
|---|---|
| 2 July | RB to Siena for the day |
| 31 Aug | Florence – Siena (1 night at inn) then to Villa Poggio al Vento, Marciano |
| 1 Oct | Back to Siena for 1 week before returning to Casa Guidi |

1851

| | |
|---|---|
| 3 May | Florence – Bologna (2 days) – Modena – Parma (1 day) – Mantua – Verona – Vicenza – Padua – Venice (Grand Canal) |
| 13 June | Left Venice – Padua (St Anthony's night) – Brescia – Milan (2 days) – Como – Lugano – Faido (1 night) – Flüelen – Lucerne (24th) – Basle – Strasbourg |
| 30 June | Arrived in Paris (Hotel aux Armes de la Ville de Paris) |
| 22 July | Left Paris for |
| 23 July | London (26 Devonshire St) |
| 25 Sept | London – Dieppe |
| 26 Sept | Dieppe – Paris (Hotel aux Armes de la Ville de Paris) |
| 10 Oct | Moved to 138 Avenue des Champs Elysées |

1852

| | |
|---|---|
| 5 July | Left Paris for |
| 6 July | London (58 Welbeck St) |
| mid-July | RB to Paris with RB Senior & Sarianna |
| 21–23 Aug | Visit to Farnham |
| Oct | Moved to 15 Bentinck St |
| 12 Oct | Left London for Paris (Hotel de la Ville l'Évêque) |

| 23 Oct | Left Paris for Châlons – Lyons (Hotel de l'Univers) – Chambéry – Lanslebourg – Susa (1 night) – Turin (2 days) – Genoa (10 days) – Pisa (1 night) – Florence (Casa Guidi) |

### 1853

| 15 July | To Bagni di Lucca (Casa Tolomei) |
| 10 Oct | Returned to Casa Guidi |
| 15 Nov | Florence – Perugia – Assisi – Terni – Rome (43 Via Bocca di Leone). 8 days' trip |

### 1854

| 28 May | Left Rome for Florence (Casa Guidi). 4/5 days' trip |

### 1855

| 13 June | To Leghorn, but missed steamer; returned to Florence, spending night of 13th at Pisa |
| 20 June | To Leghorn again, to embark for Marseilles, thence Paris |
| 24 June | Reached Paris (138 Ave des Ch. Élysées) |
| 11 July | Left Paris for |
| 12 July | London (13 Dorset St) |
| 17 Oct | Returned to Paris (102 Rue de Grenelle) |
| 13 Dec | Moved to 3 Rue du Colisée |

### 1856

| 29 June | From Paris to London (39 Devonshire Pl.) |
| 23 Aug | To Ventnor, I.o.W. |
| 6 Sept | From Ventnor to West Cowes (3 Parade) |
| 22 Sept | To Taunton |
| 30 Sept | Returned to London (39 Devonshire Pl.) |
| 23 Oct | Left London for Paris (2 days) then Marseilles |
| 28 Oct | Embarked for Genoa |
| 29 Oct | Arrived in Genoa |
| 30 Oct | Leghorn – Florence (Casa Guidi) |

### 1857

| 30 July | To Bagni di Lucca (Casa Betti) |
| 7 Oct | Left Bagni di Lucca to return to Florence (Casa Guidi) |

1858

| | |
|---|---|
| 1 July | Embarked at Leghorn |
| 3 July | Marseilles (1 night) – Hotel du Louvre |
| 4 July | Lyons (1 night) – Hotel Colet |
| 5 July | Dijon (1 night) – Hotel du Parc |
| 6 July | Arrived in Paris (Hotel de Londres, Rue Hyacinthe) |
| 19 July | Left Paris for Etretat, but settled at Le Havre (Maison Versigny, 2 Rue du Perrey) |
| 20 Sept | Left Le Havre for Paris (6 Rue de Castiglione) |
| 18 Oct | Left Paris – Mâcon (1 night) – Chambéry (2 nights) – Lanslebourg (1 night) – Susa (1 night) – Turin (1 night) – Genoa (ship overnight) – Leghorn (1 night) |
| 26 Oct | Arrived in Florence (Casa Guidi) |
| 18 Nov | Left Florence – Poggio Bagnoli (1 night) – Camuscia (1 night) – Perugia (1 night) – Spoleto (1 night) – Terni (1 night) – Città Castellana (1 night) |
| 24 Nov | Arrived in Rome (Hotel 1 night, then 43 Bocca di Leone) |

1859

| | |
|---|---|
| c 26 May | Left Rome for Florence (Casa Guidi). 4 days' trip |
| 30 July | Arrived in Siena (Hotel 2 nights) |
| 1 Aug | To Villa Alberti, Marciano (Siena) |
| 10 Oct | Returned to Florence (Casa Guidi) |
| 28 Nov | Left Florence – Poggio Bagnoli (1 night) – Passignano (1 night) – Foligno (1 night) – Terni (?2 nights) |
| 3 Dec | Arrived in Rome (Hotel d'Angleterre, then 28 Via del Tritone) |

1860

| | |
|---|---|
| 4 June | Left Rome – Viterbo (1 night) – Orvieto (1 night) – Ficulle (1 night) – Chiusi (1 night) – Siena (1 night) |
| 9 June | Arrived in Florence (Casa Guidi) |
| c 7 July | To Siena (Villa Alberti, Marciano) |
| 11 Oct | Returned to Florence (Casa Guidi) |
| c 18 Nov | Left Florence for Rome |
| 23 Nov | Arrived in Rome (126 Via Felice) |

1861

| | |
|---|---|
| c 1 June | Left Rome for Florence via Siena (1 day's rest) |
| 5 June | Arrived in Florence (Casa Guidi) |
| 29 June | E. B. B. died at Casa Guidi |
| 1 July | E. B. B. buried in Protestant Cemetery, Florence |

# Select List of Books

BIOGRAPHIES

*Elizabeth Barrett Browning, A Life*, Dorothy Hewlett (New York, 1952; Cassell & Co., London, 1953)

*The Life of Elizabeth Barrett Browning*, Gardner B. Taplin (John Murray, London, and Yale University Press, Conn., USA, 1957)

*Elizabeth Barrett Browning*, Alethea Hayter (Writers and their Work, British Council, Longmans, London, 1965)

*Mrs Browning, A Poet's Work and its Setting*, Alethea Hayter (Faber, London, 1962; Barnes and Noble, New York, 1963)

WORKS

There are numerous editions of Elizabeth Barrett Browning's work. The most recent are:

*The Poetical Works of Elizabeth Barrett Browning* (OUP, 1920)

*Complete poetical works* (Scolar Press, London 1972)

*The Complete Works of Elizabeth Barrett Browning*, edited by Charlotte Porter and Helen A. Clarke (AMS Press, New York, 1973)

*'Aurora Leigh' & Other Poems*, introduced by Cora Kaplan (The Women's Press, London, 1978)

DIARY

*The unpublished Diary of Elizabeth Barrett Browning*, 1831–1832, edited with an Introduction and Notes by Philip Kelley and Ronald Hudson. Including Psychoanalytical Observations by Robert Coles, MD (Ohio University Press, Athens, Ohio, 1969)

*The Barretts at Hope End* edited with an Introduction by Elizabeth Berridge (John Murray, London, 1974). This is an abridged version of above.

### EDITIONS OF LETTERS

A collected edition of Elizabeth Barrett Browning's letters is in preparation by Philip Kelley.

*The Letters of Elizabeth Barrett Browning*, edited with biographical additions by F. G. Kenyon, 2 vols (Smith Elder & Co., London, 1897; Macmillan, New York, 1897 and 1899)

*Letters of Elizabeth Barrett Browning Addressed to Richard Hengist Horne*, edited by S. R. T. Mayer, 2 vols (R. Bentley, 1876/7)

*Letters to Robert Browning and Other Correspondents by Elizabeth Barrett Browning*, edited by Thomas J. Wise (London, 1915)

*The Letters of Robert Browning and Elizabeth Barrett Browning, 1845–46*, edited by Elvan Kintner (Cambridge, Mass., 1909)

*Letters to her sisters, 1846–59*, edited by Leonard Huxley (John Murray, London, 1929; E. P. Dutton, New York, 1930)

*Letters from Elizabeth Barrett to B. R. Haydon*, edited by Martha Hale Shackford (OUP, Oxford and New York, 1939)

*Invisible Friends: the Correspondence of Benjamin Robert Haydon, 1842–1845*, edited by W. B. Pope (Cambridge, Mass., 1972)

*Letters of the Brownings to George Barrett*, edited by Paul Landis and Ronald Freeman (University of Illinois Press, 1958)

*Letters from Elizabeth Barrett Browning to Miss Mitford*, edited and introduced by Betty Miller (John Murray, London, 1954; Yale, New Haven, Conn., 1954)

*Letters from Elizabeth Barrett Browning to Hugh Stuart Boyd*, edited by Barbara P. McCarthy (Murray, London, 1955; Yale, New Haven, Conn., 1955)

*The Love Letters of Robert Browning and Elizabeth Barrett*, selected by V. E. Stack (Heinemann, London, 1969)

*Elizabeth Barrett Browning's Letters to Mrs David Ogilvy, 1849–1861*, edited by Peter N. Haydon and Philip Kelley (The Browning Institute, New York, 1973; John Murray, London, 1974)

### MISCELLANEOUS

*The English in Italy*, G. S. Hillard (Boston, 1853)

*William Wetmore Story and His Friends* by Henry James, 2 vols (Houghton, Mifflin, Boston, 1903; Blackwood, Edinburgh, 1903)

*E.B.B. in her Letters*, Percy Lubbock (Smith, Elder, London, 1906)

*The Stuffed Owl*, D. Bevan, Wyndham Lewis, C. Lee (Dent, London, 1930)

*Flush*, Virginia Woolf (Hogarth Press, London, 1933)

*The Family of the Barretts, A Colonial Romance*, Jeanette Marks (Macmillan Co., New York, 1938)

# SELECT LIST OF BOOKS

*The Athenaeum, A Mirror of Victorian Culture*, Leslie A. Marchand (Chapel Hill, North Carolina, 1941)

*Owen Meredith*, Aurelia Brooks Harlan (Columbia University Press, New York, 1946)

*Landor, A Replevin*, Malcolm Elwin (Macdonald, London, 1958)

*Sublime and Instructive*, Virginia Surtees (Michael Joseph, London, 1972)

*Creative Malady*, Sir George Pickering (Allen & Unwin, London, 1974)

*Lord Leighton*, Leonée and Richard Ormond (Yale and Mellon Foundation, 1975)

*The Brownings and Mrs. Kinney, a Record of their Friendship*, Ronald W. Bosco, *Browning Institute Studies*, Vol. 4 (New York, 1976)

*The Brownings' Correspondence, A Checklist*, Philip Kelley, Ronald Hudson (The Browning Institute, New York; Wedgestone Press, Kansas, 1978)

*My Browning Album*, Vivienne Browning (Springwood Books, London, 1979)

*The Brownings at Casa Guidi*, Edward C. McAleer (The Browning Institute, New York, 1979)

## JOURNALS

*Country Life*, Vol. CXLIV (London, 19 September 1968)

*Princeton University Library Chronicle* (1972)

Various volumes of *Browning Institute Studies* and *Newsletters* from Armstrong Browning Library, Waco, Texas

# Acknowledgments

I am very grateful to Philip Kelley for his encouragement to me in embarking on this book and for directing me to unpublished material, particularly the *Memoir* by Sophia Cottrell, and letters from Elizabeth Barrett Browning which will appear in his edition of the Brownings' correspondence. He has also allowed me to reproduce from his *Checklist* the very useful table of the Brownings' travels.

I should also like to thank Elaine Baly (Vivienne Browning), President of the Browning Society, London, for many references, and the Browning Institute of America for co-operation.

Katherine Macdonald has most generously allowed me to use extracts from unpublished letters from Elizabeth Barrett Browning and Robert Browning to her grandfather, the sculptor, Alexander Munro.

I am much indebted to Christopher Falkus for his helpful comments on the first draft of the MS.

The firm of John Murray has kindly given me copyright permissions, as have Edward Moulton-Barrett and Mary V. Altham.

I should like to thank Mary Lutyens for the loan of books about her grandfather, 'Owen Meredith', 1st Earl of Lytton; Virginia Surtees for information about Ellen Heaton and much else; Ivor Bulmer-Thomas for correcting the accents on my Greek; Renée Tickell for offering particulars about the medium Home from the archives of the SPR; Marjorie Jones for discussions and loan of books; Mavis Batey of the Garden History Society for particulars about J. C. Loudon; Leonard R. Denis of Philadelphia and Margaret Cole of Hofstra University, Long Island, New York, for tracing illustrations from American sources.

I very much appreciate the generous hospitality of John and Patricia Hegarty in showing me round Hope End, where they have converted the original stables into a small private hotel and are working on restoring the grounds as far as possible as the Barretts would have known them.

I am also grateful to Professor Robert Martin; Vincent Quinn, Librarian of Balliol College, Oxford; Dr John Leedham-Green; Hilda Clark; K. Fletcher; John Curtis, Barbara Gough, and Annabel Jenkins; Ann Darby for her patience and skill in deciphering my MS.; and to Monty Smith, Curator at Wightwick, for intercepting many interruptions.

I much appreciate the ready consent given to me to use material in the following collections:

The Armstrong Browning Library, Baylor University, Waco, Texas, for copyright permissions; Dr Herring, Director, has most kindly and promptly sent me copies of publications.

The New York Public Library for material from the Henry W. and Albert A. Berg Collection, Astor, Lenox and Tilden Foundations; I am indebted to the Curator, Dr Lola L. Szladits, for co-operation over many years.

Manuscripts and pictures in the English Poetry Collection Library, Wellesley College Library, Wellesley, Mass. The Special Collections Librarian, Dr Eleanor Nicholes, was most hospitable to me during my visit there in 1978.

A note of appreciation is due, as ever, to the staff of the London Library who never fail in their much-tried courtesy to members unable to find what they want in the catalogue or in sections sometimes misleadingly labelled (why do 'Cats' and 'Women' come under 'Science'?), or on awkwardly placed bottom shelves. These have become increasingly difficult-to-get-up-from since the days when I was the student deputed to fetch books for the library of Queen's College, Harley Street, London.

The author and publishers would like to thank the following for their kind permission to reproduce material in their possession: English Poetry Collection Library, Wellesley College, Wellesley, Mass., for the title page of *Poems, 1844* and the bust by W. W. Story; the Historical Society of Pennsylvania, Philadelphia, for the portrait by Buchanan Read; the Fitzwilliam Museum, Cambridge, for the portrait by D. G. Rossetti; the Huntington Library, San Marino, California, for the sketch by Thackeray; the Armstrong Browning Library, Baylor University, Waco, Texas, for the bust of Penini and portrait by E. F. Bridell; the National Portrait Gallery, London, for portraits by Field Talfourd and Michele Gordigiani, and the Tate Gallery, London, for 'This was a Piedmontese' by Arthur Hughes.

# Index